HOW TO HOMESCHOOL IN CANADA

A TRAVEL GUIDE FOR YOUR HOMESCHOOLING JOURNEY

LISA MARIE FLETCHER

THE CANADIAN HOMESCHOOLER

Cover design by Joy Kenney © 2020

ISBN: 978-1-772978-1-7 (ebook)

ISBN: 978-1-7772978-0-0 (print)

"It is good to have an end to journey toward,

but it is the journey that matters in the end."

- Ursula K. Le Guin

ACKNOWLEDGEMENTS

First and foremost, I want to thank my husband, Jonathan, for putting up with all my crazy ideas and my children for being very understanding while I've been busy.

Thank you, Monique and Shari. What you do to help me stay focused has been one of the major reasons I've been able to get things done.

Then there's my writing posse - Charlotte, Chris, and Tristan - who remind me that every word counts when it comes to putting ideas to paper.

Thank you to my sister-in-law, Joy, for the beautiful cover design for this book, and to Bonnie for helping me polish this to a finished product.

A huge thank you to my homeschooling community and readers who have been supportive of everything.

Finally, thank you for picking up this book. I hope it helps you start this journey with confidence.

TABLE OF CONTENTS

HOMESCHOOL IS A JOURNEY

Welcome to the Canadian Homeschooling Outfitter Shop. My name is Lisa Marie and I'll be your trail guide on this homeschooling adventure. I'm so excited to have you join me here. Together, we will kick off this homeschool journey with confidence and excitement.

Have you ever been on a big adventure?

When I was 19, my best friend and I decided we would head to Britain and backpack around for a month. Before we got started, our first step was to borrow as many travel guides from the library as possible, research everything we could about the places we wanted to visit, learn about every youth hostel in the whole country, and come up with a detailed itinerary of our plan. We sat in on sessions held by experienced travelers and took notes of things we would need to bring with us. Gleaning wisdom was our new favourite pastime.

Then we visited our local outfitter shop to get our supplies, like fancy backpacks (mine had a detachable day pack!) and sleeping bags that take up hardly any space. We listened to the advice of the staff for what resources we needed for this adventure and, several attempts at packing and repacking later, we stood in the airport waving goodbye to our parents. I remember being so excited but really nervous at the same time.

We had done all our research and knew what we were up to but still, there was that small bit of uncertainty about what lay ahead. We landed in London, England, and felt completely overwhelmed by a massive city with so many people and customs we didn't fully know. It took us a while to find our bearings and make our way to the hostel we had booked for the night. We were in over our heads, but ready for the adventure of a lifetime.

It wasn't until we got out of the city that we found our stride - learning to adapt our plan to the moment and the things we discovered along the way. I'm so glad we did. Some of the best moments of our whole trip happened in those unplanned moments. Like the time we spontaneously jumped off the train in a little town and followed a path along the edge of a cliff close enough to nearly pet the sheep in the field. (I still have a small handful of wool we collected from the bushes.) That trail led to a breathtaking castle ruin overlooking the ocean. We spent the rest of the day there, just daydreaming.

When we got home, we were changed. Our days of travelling had fueled our passion for adventure. It was a time I will never forget.

So, what does my trip to Britain have to do with a book about homeschooling?

I always refer homeschooling to a journey when people ask me for advice or support. The more and more I thought about that, the more I realized it really is a journey. Let me explain.

In our adventure to Britain, our very first step was to learn everything we could so we knew what we were getting ourselves into. And look - you're doing the same thing right now! We wanted that base knowledge so we could be prepared for what laid ahead, just like you do.

Next, we went and got all the things we needed - our backpacks and supplies. The outfitters' shop was a key to getting ready to go. There is a picture in my head of a log cabin-style outfitter shop where people thinking of homeschooling arrive to get geared up for their journey. This is the first stop on the homeschool adventure - finding resources, understanding more about what they are embarking on, making sure they have everything they need and grabbing a map of the journey ahead. It's a chance to meet up with other people who are also heading out, gleaning wisdom and experience from those who have walked the trail already.

When the backpacks are loaded up and the hiking shoes are tied on tight, we are ready to get going.

The start of a homeschooling journey can feel like our arrival in a big city. The hustle and bustle of people just doing their thing, using lingo you might not understand at first, is overwhelming. But once you get going, you settle in, learning what works and what doesn't and getting more comfortable with adapting on the fly. That allows you to enjoy the adventure so much more.

IN THE MEADOW

If you start homeschooling from the beginning, you step out of the outfitters' shop and make your way to a rustic-looking wooden sign with the word "adventure" carved into its face, which guides to you the trail.

(Don't worry if you are starting somewhere else on the path. You get to be one of those adventurers who joins the group by helicopter!)

In front of you is a wide, green meadow. A rainbow of flowers splatters between the blades of grass, waving gently in the warm breeze. The initial path fades a few steps in, allowing you to wander and explore at your leisure. You can stop and lay in the grass to find shapes in the clouds. You can curl up in the shade of a single over-sized maple tree to rest. You can pick flowers, or just simply stand in the middle of everything, breathing in the nearly overpowering smell of nature. There is time to enjoy every step and wondrous moment.

This is preschool.

There is no need to rush to the end of the meadow. You are free to take your time and enjoy these early years.

If you have decided to homeschool and you have a young child, you might be wondering how to homeschool preschool. You might be feeling a sense of overwhelm and confusion as you look for options and information. Preschool doesn't have to be complicated. You don't need a full curriculum to be successful; you just need to have fun with your kids.

THROUGH THE FOREST

Tall trees tower at the edge of the grassy landscape of the early years. As you stand there, craning your neck to look up at the tops of the trees and peering into what feels like darkness, you may feel intimidated about stepping into such a place.

At first, the trees are sparse, wide-spread enough that you can wander without a real path. As you make your way farther in, you see a faint wide path emerging in the dirt beneath your feet, guiding you through the trees as they start to become closer together.

The vibrant colours of the leaves and underbrush make this part of the journey beautiful. Sunlight streams in somehow to light the way. The sound of the wind rustling above you makes you pause and enjoy the moment.

These are the elementary school years: Grades 1 through 5.

Often that first step into something "official" can feel intimidating. Whether you start from the edge of the forest or get dropped into the middle, it takes some time to get your bearings.

Just like the meadow of preschool, the first few elementary years still allow for much flexibility and exploration through play and curiosity. As you move towards the end of this period of learning, you will find your work tends to become more intentional and focused, but not heavily so - there is still plenty of room to wander.

In these elementary years, it's important to continue keeping school fun and engaging to develop that love of learning. At this point, it is still mostly you as the parent who is setting the personal and academic goals for your child.

The best thing about homeschooling in these elementary years is that they are very well supported. Plenty of curriculum and resources are available for you, especially focusing on the development of foundational skills like reading, writing, and arithmetic.

OVER THE HILLS

Pushing your way out of the treeline, you now enter the foothills of learning. You need to make your way over the ups and downs of this hilly region, no matter how much the inclines make your thighs ache.

The view from here is beautiful. Trees behind you, mountains ahead. There's a path here. One that keeps going in the right direction so you don't stumble and find yourself sinking up to your knees in mud or tumbling down a steep edge.

Between trying to keep your footing, nerves about what lies ahead, and struggling to keep pushing forward, these hills can be a challenge.

The foothills of high school are the middle school years of grades 6 through 8. This time is a combination of puberty and personal independence with a tendency to become much more intentional and focused. At this point, most families are thinking ahead to the looming adventure that is high school and making plans for what comes next. Curriculum, if used, often becomes more difficult and heavy, developing the skills they will need later on.

UP THE MOUNTAINS

Mountain climbing involves a lot of planning, skill, and effort. Special tools and prep work are needed to reach the summit. Now, your footwork matters - careful steps into specific places, even though the way you climb to the top might not follow the same path as everyone else. You have to focus because a single slip could be the difference between success and failure. The view, if you remember to take time to look around and see, is beautiful. Looking up, you can glimpse the summit just ahead - an exciting conclusion to the end of a homeschool journey.

These are the high school years. Grades 9 through 12 are the period of learning where everything comes together with intention and focus. You need to have some kind of goal or plan for these years, although your plan might not look the same as anyone else's.

At this point, your child should be able to do much of their work with some level of independence. In some ways, you are now the belay hooks in the rock - the clips that a mountain climber attaches their ropes to so that if they fall, they don't plummet back to the bottom. Instead, they are caught at the last place they hooked into. It's your job to keep them on the path and focused on their goals.

Learning is very intentional and focused. Curriculum is a combination of core subjects and electives with a path planned out to help your student reach the top of their goals.

AT THE SUMMIT

You made it.

Sitting here at the top of the mountain, you can see clearly behind you - the entire journey from start to finish, including that tiny building far off on the horizon: the outfitter's shop that began this whole adventure. Whether you started in the meadow or helicoptered in along the path, you can take this time to look back over the trail and appreciate everything you've accomplished.

Ahead of you, the world awaits your freshly graduated teen. From here, they get to choose which path they take for their life, knowing you are sitting there cheering them on.

It's a beautiful sight.

One of the best things is that you can now turn around and encourage people still on the path behind you. Be a mentor. Take your turn being the trail guide and help those making their way along this journey.

THE TRAIL GUIDE

A great thing about homeschooling is that you don't have to do it alone. Just like adventurers, you can follow in the footsteps of someone who has been there and done that. A trail guide can offer the experience of their own journey, help you get connected with the support and resources you need, encourage you when you struggle to keep up, and set you back on track if you wander off the path.

I am your trail guide. With more than a decade of homeschool experience behind me and many more ahead, I've been walking this trail from that first day in the outfitter's shop when I felt like you - overwhelmed, anxious, and eager to get started.

Ready to go? Let me show you around the shop so we can head out on our homeschooling journey together.

YOUR ACTION STEP

Throughout this book, you will find action steps at the end of many chapters. Doing these steps will help you plan and prepare to have the foundations for a great homeschool year.

PART I:

BEFORE YOU GET STARTED

CHAPTER ONE

WHAT IS YOUR WHY?

When my eldest son was old enough to go to Junior Kindergarten, an uneasy feeling settled into my stomach as I put his name on the school list. I traipsed across the street to sit in the cute little classroom and learn more about how a typical day in these early years happened. That experience left me with a vivid memory of colourful posters on the walls, tiny coat cubbies, and a file folder of printables to take home with more information and activities we could do together.

I sat down with my little guy, a fat pencil, and a pair of kid-friendly scissors. He loved it and I figured he would do great at school.

My son had other ideas. Anxiety hit hard. I found him hiding from me frequently, especially if we talked about school. He started clinging to me, afraid I would leave him. Toilet training became a nightmare when he regressed unexpectedly. The more I watched, the more he shrank.

That decided it for us. I figured we'd stay home for the year and decide what to do the following year. I chose to respect that he wasn't ready for school yet. As soon as we freed him from the stress of having to go to school, my son thrived - and so did I.

Even after a few years of successfully homeschooling, a few conversations with people who disapproved left me reeling a little. I started doubting my choices and feeling rather incompetent. So I sat down and thought about why I chose homeschooling as our education plan.

Honestly, I should have done that from the very beginning.

The very first step every homeschooler should take is to know the reasons why you are homeschooling.

Knowing the WHY behind your choice to homeschool makes it easier for you to explain and refute that decision when questioned. More importantly, it gives you something to reaffirm your choice if or when you have times of doubt or challenges.

Each family has their own reasons for choosing to homeschool. After years of talking with families, I've noticed that many reasons fall into these main categories:

- To offer an education that better lines up with your religious or moral beliefs
- Disapproval of or dissatisfaction with the school system's curriculum, methods, agenda, environment, ability to meet your child's needs, etc.
- Bullying or other social challenges
- Medical needs or special needs such as illness, autism, allergies, ADD, learning disabilities, etc. that would be better handled from home
- Lifestyle choices, such as travelling, sports/acting, or living in a foreign country

Of course, this list is in no way definitive, and most of the time there is a combination of reasons families choose to homeschool.

For our family, many reasons fueled our decision to homeschool: values we wanted to instill in our children, my desire to be with my children every day, struggles with bullying in our own school years that we didn't want repeated, and the desire to let us go at the pace that my children set - not the one set out for them.

When you are thinking about why you homeschool (or plan to homeschool), don't forget to ask your child. It's amazing how much insight they can offer into the reasons why you choose to learn at home.

Our decision to keep my son home from Junior Kindergarten turned into a grand adventure. Today, that boy is a teenager, taller than I am, well into his high school years and still happily learning at home.

Over the years, our reasons have flowed and changed. It's one of the beautiful things about homeschooling. It adapts to your life.

Make sure that as your journey progresses, you take a moment to pause and revisit this step. Re-evaluate your reasons why to keep yourself on track and encouraged to keep moving forward.

Think about it carefully. It makes a difference to be confident when deciding to do something that is essentially counter-cultural. It's easier to throw in the towel if the WHY isn't clear or you can't remember it.

YOUR ACTION STEP

Take some time and write all of your reasons down. When done, put the list somewhere you can see it regularly. It's a great reminder and an encouragement to keep going.

CHAPTER TWO
THE LEGAL STUFF

Although homeschooling in Canada is completely legal, each province and territory has its own set of regulations and expectations surrounding home education. It is your responsibility to familiarize yourself with what your province/territory requires. The last thing you want is to have a conflict that could cause big troubles for your family and your intent to educate at home.

Laws change frequently. Your best solution to making sure you complete the requirements needed is to connect with the homeschool association in your province or on your province's education department's website.

Below is a basic summary of what is expected in each province or territory. Please keep in mind that this is not official legal advice and, even in the process of putting this book together, requirements changed for various provinces. Be diligent and confirm for yourself what is needed before you start.

British Columbia

In British Columbia, there are 2 main options for learning at home. One is distributed learning (enrolling) and the other is homeschooling (registering.) There is a big difference between the two, registering being more independent whereas distributed learning requires you to meet specific provincial learning outcomes.

Homeschoolers in BC get some financial support, with the value dependent on what option is chosen.

Visit the BC Home Educator's Association (BCHEA) for more information: https://bchea.ca/

Alberta

In Alberta, families who homeschool are required to register with a willing board somewhere in the province and have their plans approved.

Options include:

- completely doing your own plans (traditional)
- following some of the government curriculum outlines (shared responsibility)
- completely following the school plans (distance education)

With these options, you are a) assigned a facilitator who visits you throughout the year, and b) offered funding, depending on what school board and method of schooling you choose.

A fourth option added in the fall of 2020 allows parents to send in an annual notification along with an education plan for an unsupervised, notification-only, non-funded home education choice.

For more information, visit Alberta Home Education Association (AHEA) at www.aheaonline.com or the Alberta Homeschooling Association at albertahomeschooling.ca.

Saskatchewan

Homeschoolers in Saskatchewan are required to register with their school board and provide an educational plan for each child. Throughout the year, they need to keep a portfolio of work or provide a written summary which they present at the end of the year. Funding for homeschoolers varies according to district.

Visit the Saskatchewan Home Based Educators (SHBE) for more information: www.shbe.info.

Manitoba

In Manitoba, homeschoolers need to inform the government they are homeschooling. In January, and again in June, an official report is filed outlining the learning completed. This province offers no funding to homeschooling families.

For more information, visit the Manitoba Association of Christian Home Schools (MACHS) at machs.ca or the Manitoba Association for Schooling at Home (MASH) at manitobahomeschool.com.

Ontario

Ontario homeschoolers are asked to submit a yearly letter of intent to their local school board. There is no other requirement or involvement from the government. This province offers no funding to homeschooling families.

Visit the Ontario Federation of Teaching Parents (OFTP) at ontariohomeschool.org or the Ontario Christian Home-Educator's Connection (OCHEC) at www.ochec.org for more information.

Québec

This province has some of the most detailed regulations and requirements for homeschooling, and regulations change frequently. Current requirements include sending in written notification, submission of a learning plan, meeting with a facilitator, and reports throughout the year.

Please connect with a homeschool association in the province for complete details about what is required. Québec offers no funding to homeschooling families.

Association québécoise pour l'éducation à domicile (AQED) is the best support resource for new homeschoolers. Find their website at www.aqed.qc.ca.

New Brunswick

In New Brunswick, homeschooling families have to either register with an English or a French board. This requires submission of a fairly basic set of forms to which you will receive a letter of approval. This province offers no funding to homeschooling families.

Visit the Home Educators of New Brunswick (HENB) at henb.ca for more information.

Nova Scotia

In Nova Scotia, parents are required to register their child using a form available on the Ministry of Education's website. In June, parents need to follow that up with a progress report, outlining what their child learned throughout the year. This province offers no funding to homeschooling families.

Visit the Nova Scotia Home Education Association (NHSEA) at www.nshea.org or Helping Encouraging Mentoring Service (HEMS) at hems-ns.ca for more information.

Prince Edward Island

All that is required for PEI homeschoolers is to fill out and submit a notice of intent form. This province offers no funding to homeschooling families.

There is no provincial association in Prince Edward Island. Information can be found on the government's website at www.princeedwardisland.ca/en/information/education-and-lifelong-learning/home-education.

Newfoundland & Labrador

Parents/guardians must apply by June for the upcoming school year. Students will be registered in their community school. Progress reports are required up to 3 times a year depending on how long you've been homeschooling. This province offers no funding to homeschooling families.

There is no provincial association in Newfoundland and Labrador. Information can be found on the government's website at www.gov.nl.ca/eecd/k12/homeschooling.

Northwest Territories

In the Northwest Territories, parents register their children with their local school, where they are classified as students but are exempt from attendance. Homeschoolers in this province get a portion of the funding from the school to help pay for their school expenses.

There is no homeschool association in the NWT. The Home Schooling Directive is available at https://www.ece.gov.nt.ca/sites/ece/files/resources/home_schooling.pdf.

Nunavut

Homeschooling in Nunavut involves registering with a local school and working with the leadership in that school. Inclusion of Inuit Qaujimajatuqangit (IQ) or the teaching of Inuit societal values and culture is to be included in your homeschool education plans. Funding in this province is available on a reimbursement plan.

There is no homeschooling association in this territory. Homeschooling regulations are outlined in section 21 of the Education Act found at www.nunatsiaqonline.ca/pub/docs/e2008snc15.pdf

Yukon

Yukon homeschoolers need to register with the Aurora Virtual School, who coordinates the home education program for Yukon Education for Anglophones or École Nomade for Francophones. Along with registration, you need to submit a home education plan that outlines the plans and learning outcomes for the year divided into four semesters. The Yukon uses the British Columbia curriculum outline for their guidelines. Funding is provided for homeschoolers in this province.

You can find out more at the Aurora Virtual School website at www.auroravirtualschool.ca/home-education.html.

HSLDA Canada

In Canada, we have access to a resource known as the Homeschool Legal Defence Association of Canada (HSLDA Canada). In their own words, here is what they offer:

> "HSLDA's mission is to enable, empower, and protect Canadian home educators. As such, our strong desire is to make a difference in the homeschooling community at large by being a positive influence in the lives of individual families. Our name indicates our unique and primary role: we are our members' defence and assurance in any legal matters that might impact their ability and right to homeschool (including letters to government organizations, jury duty exemption, court cases, and provincial notification forms).
>
> We are actively involved in provincial, federal, and international politics to ensure that Canadians' constitutional freedoms to homeschool are not limited or jeopardized.
>
> However, what many people do not realize is that our members experience many other benefits as well. Membership to HSLDA provides insurance coverage over homeschooling events and activities. As well, HSLDA is committed not only to defending your freedom to homeschool, but also to lightening your load as you homeschool. Our expert staff, our member site, our social media sites, and our regular emails are full of insight, resources, and answers to help our members in their homeschool journey.
>
> From preschool to high school graduation to entering the post-secondary realm, HSLDA has the knowledge and help that you need to homeschool well. You do not need to wait for a crisis: you can contact our office anytime with questions you may have."

Membership with the HSLDA is not required to homeschool, although some families feel it is a vital part of their homeschooling basics. You will have to decide if the HSLDA is something that lines up with your family's values or needs. You can find out more about their program at hslda.ca.

YOUR ACTION STEP

Take some time to understand the legal requirements of the province or territory you live in and complete the requirements to get started.

CHAPTER THREE
DESCHOOLING

One of the hardest things about homeschooling is our preconceived ideas of what education should be like, especially since most of us have been through the school system ourselves. We have been trained to think school needs to consist of specific things, subjects need to be taught a specific way, tests need to be done to verify learning, and we have to make sure certain outcomes are reached at specific times.

The thing is, homeschooling breaks all those rules. The whole point of home education is to embrace the freedom to educate how you want. While you can choose to do things similarly to the classroom setting, it's still going to be different.

Homeschooling is a lifestyle - not just an education.

You might hear the word "deschooling" mentioned by veteran homeschoolers, especially if you are pulling your child out of the school system.

Deschooling is when you take time off from the mindset and structured life of public schooling. If your child has had a rough experience in school, time will be needed to recover from that. If your decision to homeschool was made abruptly, you will need time to shift gears.

The challenging part of this experience is your personal expectations of education and learning. It's hard to let go, even for a little while. Spend time with your child and get to know them better before getting into the plans of homeschooling. This break gives your child a chance to decompress and reset their educational experience, and honestly, it's just as much for you, the parent.

It's incredibly freeing when you pass through that barrier of what you think education needs to be like.

Deschooling means dropping all formal education and letting your kids be free to do whatever they want for a while; allow them to be aimless, be okay with them doing nothing all day, leave them to play, explore, and pursue their interests without the pressure of school. During this time, you can still have learning experiences together.

- Go on field trips. Museums and galleries are open during the day and often aren't that busy because people are at work or school. Take advantage of that opportunity and discover some great places in your community or take a day trip and head to the nearest major city to visit some of their sites.

- Watch documentaries or TED talks. There are so many interesting video resources that inspire curiosity and discussion. Find topics that appeal to your child and watch them together.

- Read. Whether they read comic books or classics, 1 book or 100 - reading is a great tool to use in this time. You can even try snuggling on a couch together and reading a book aloud so you can discuss what you are reading. If the book has a movie version, watch it together and talk about the differences.

- Get outside. Fresh air does wonders. Try things like geocaching, step counting challenges, and going for walks. Take a tree/bird identification guide with you.

- Play games. Board games like Scrabble, Monopoly, and even poker offer great learning opportunities without the pressure of school. There are many different websites full of educational games that are just plain fun. Even console games can sneak math and language into your day.

- Bake (or cook, or clean, or do laundry). Every day housework develops important life skills. They all require attention to detail and following instructions, and math is often built right in.

- Order a subscription box or activity kit. Getting something fun to do in the mail is exciting. There are so many options to choose from - pick a box that interests your child.

This is also a great time to connect with other homeschoolers. Find a group or family near you to meet up with and spend time together. If your child can build that firm foundation of friendship with someone else, it will help make the transition easier.

You may be wondering how long you should spend deschooling. As with everything related to homeschooling, it will depend on your family. A general rule is to give your child at least 1 month per grade that they've been in school.

Of course, you know your child best. If you see they are ready to sit down and start learning more formally, move ahead to make choices for what's next. However, don't push too soon or you might find yourself headbutting more than learning.

YOUR ACTION STEP

Spend some time considering what your preconceptions are about education and school. Figure out how long you need to deschool your child for and come up with some unique learning experiences you can do together outside of the usual classroom model.

CHAPTER FOUR

FINDING A SUPPORT SYSTEM

Imagine yourself in the middle of the forest after hiking all day. Your legs ache from all the walking. Your favourite hiking shirt drips with sweat. Blisters cover your feet. The pack on your back feels like it weighs a million pounds, breathing is more like gasping, and you wonder if you've lost the path because every direction looks the same. Needing to walk for another hour to get to camp feels impossible.

Now, imagine a friend coming up behind you with a bright smile and an encouraging word of "almost there." They offer to carry your pack for a while so you can get your breathing back under control, and the compass in their hand points in the direction you have to go. Suddenly, that last hour of work feels much more attainable. Together, you press on, finally making it to camp where you can relax for the night.

That is the reason you need a support system.

During your homeschooling journey, you are going to hit periods that just feel hard. You will need someone to come alongside you, speak an encouraging word, and help you get through that rough stretch.

Having support is an essential key to your homeschooling success.

A homeschool support group traditionally consists of several homeschool families that get together in person for various meetings or events. This group provides opportunities for kids to interact with other homeschooled kids, for parents to connect socially, and for the group to get access to things like field trips or classes.

The benefits of an in-person support group may include:

- social opportunities for both kids and parents

- field trip opportunities (and sometimes group discounts!)

- someone to "talk shop" with about curriculum, methods, learning styles, etc.

- encouragement from other people with the same experiences

- people who have your back against opposition

- wisdom and experience from veteran homeschoolers

- the resale of curriculum and resources between members

In today's technological world, support groups aren't just limited to the homeschoolers in your local community. We can connect with families from around the world through online groups, opening up a whole new set of support networks that didn't exist all that long ago. We're able to find people from all walks of life who are experiencing the same day-to-day struggles, successes, and questions we have.

When you are trying to find a support group for your homeschooling experience, you want to ideally find people who are going through the same kind of journey as you. Although similar geographic location is a good place to start, don't be afraid to think outside the box. This can be an amazing asset to families who find themselves in a minority in their local community, have specific challenges, or choose to homeschool in a way that's not common.

For example,

- If you are homeschooling a child with special needs of any sort, search for a group around that need.

- Look for a group that is built around the same faith (or non-faith) as you.

- Check for a group based on the grade ranges/genders/interests of your child(ren).

- Find a group that is using the same curriculum choices or homeschooling method as you.

But you might be wondering - where do you find these homeschooling communities?

Facebook is a favourite hangout for many homeschoolers as it's easy to interact with each other. If you have an active Facebook account, type the name of your city or region into the search bar along with the word "homeschool." You can usually find a list of local groups.

Be sure to search for a provincial or even a national group. Often these communities offer connections to smaller, active groups to get involved with — or at least point you in a good direction.

You can also look up your province's homeschool support website and see if they have a list of groups near you.

If you are looking for local homeschoolers, check the library, art gallery, swimming pool, or YMCA. See if they have classes available for homeschooling families. Show up during class time to connect one-on-one, and have a conversation to discover what support groups are around.

A couple of years ago, our family moved to a smaller town. When I popped into the library to get some new cards, I ended up talking to the librarian for a while. In our conversation, homeschooling came up. Before I knew it, I was connected to the leader of the local homeschooling group! Use the networking available to you to meet people.

YOUR ACTION STEP

Look for homeschoolers in your community and get connected - either online or in person.

CHAPTER FIVE

ANSWERING COMMON QUESTIONS

There are a million questions that run through our heads when we first start thinking about homeschooling. We want the best for our children, so making this decision can weigh heavily on our thoughts. Let's answer a few of the main questions.

NECESSARY QUALIFICATIONS?

What qualifications do you need to teach your children?

Because teachers are required to have an education degree to teach in a school, there's a common curiosity about whether homeschool parents need some training too. The answer is no.

Teachers are taught methodology, evaluation techniques, child development, classroom management, and other skills important to running a classroom full of children smoothly and effectively. Homeschooling parents typically don't need any of the same skills.

We have some advantages that can't be found in a traditional classroom, such as:

- smaller "class sizes" so our teacher/student ratio is much better
- the ability to outsource any subjects we need help with
- learning along with our kids when needed
- seeing their successes and weaknesses first-hand
- personalizing lessons based on their learning styles and interests
- going as fast or as slow as we want based on their needs.

WHAT ABOUT SOCIALIZATION?

If you venture into the world with nothing more than a plane ticket and the pack on your back, it could feel lonely. Landing in a new country can be a nerve-wracking, especially if you don't know anyone.

But the awesome thing? You meet people. You connect up with other backpackers and start travelling together. You get to know the locals if you stay in one place for a while. You learn the customs and language. It's not a life of isolation, but a fantastic opportunity to interact with a wide variety of people.

This experience is similar to homeschooling.

Socialization is defined as how to behave in our society and communities: culturally, emotionally, and responsibly. It teaches us how to act.

Do you remember being in school and hearing a teacher say, "You aren't here to socialize!"? The truth is that school was never designed to be a social activity. It's intended to be an educational activity. So why do people generally think school is the place for optimal socialization?

> *Don't worry about socialization. Wherever people congregate, there is going to be interaction and socialization. Where is it written that it needs to be in schools? ~ Mary Kay Clarke.*

Honestly, I don't think this is what people mean when they ask about socialization. I think they want to know how homeschooled kids find friends.

School offers an easy solution for making friends because it forces kids into smaller communities to interact every day. The difference with homeschooling is that while homeschooling offers plenty of opportunities to socialize, it has to be done with intent.

Yes, you are going to hear examples of that "awkward homeschooled kid." People have different personalities. There are awkward, shy, and introverted people in every walk of life. There is no reason whatsoever to believe that a child who has been homeschooled is going to be unable to handle social norms.

Homeschoolers generally don't stay locked up in their homes and never venture out into the world. Most of them are actively involved with others: taking part in homeschooling groups, classes, activities, and programs. They join extra-curricular clubs like Scouts and cadets and sports teams. They play at the playground, go to the store, and interact with neighbours and friends. They are part of the communities they live in. Participating in the actions of day to day life affords plenty of time and opportunity to interact with people.

Homeschooling groups are often inclusive of a variety of age groups, from babies to teens. Kids enjoy playing with and making friends with people of all ages. Many can hold conversations with grown-ups in a respectful and engaging way.

As long as we offer chances for our kids to learn and develop those social skills of behaving in the world, we are doing fine. Kids are smart; they pick up necessary skills quickly. It doesn't take long for homeschooled kids to realize they need to put their hands up to speak in a group setting or stand in a line when needed. It's not a school that teaches them that. It's the opportunities they have with people in their everyday experience.

WHAT IF WE FALL BEHIND?

Taking a journey is hard work. There are going to be times where you make great strides and progress towards the end goal, and days when you have to force yourself to put one foot in front of the other.

Homeschooling is hard work, too. There may be times when you are looking at people ahead of you on the path and wondering if you are falling behind.

In school, each step of the process is guided with levels and expectations for success. There are markers to reach and learning outcomes to achieve. It makes things predictable and measurable - especially for teachers who have a whole classroom full of children to evaluate. This means if you don't reach a specific outcome, you may be considered behind. Think of it as a camp at the end of a hike for the day. If the expectation is that you will arrive at 2 pm, but you drag yourself in at 6 pm - you will be behind. It's the same idea.

The difference with homeschooling is that we aren't usually governed by these same checkpoints. There is no need to feel behind because we can adjust the expectations to our child instead. We don't have the obligation of timelines like school does.

As a homeschooler, it is incredibly challenging not to compare your children to other kids their age or to the pre-ordained checklist of things they "should" know by a specific age.

One of the hardest things to grasp is that you don't usually have to follow the provincial standards. Sure, you can use those learning outcomes as a guideline for what to aim for, but every child learns at their own pace. They will excel at some things and struggle with others — and that's okay. If there are areas of weakness, you can focus on those weaker areas as needed to help them reach a higher potential.

Working at their own speed means you have your child's best interests at heart. This is one of the major reasons homeschooling is a fantastic way to educate your child. The most important thing is that you are still putting one foot in front of the other and making progress. It doesn't matter what speed you get there.

WHAT ABOUT UNIVERSITY?

This question gets asked a lot — even if the child in question is only in preschool! We all want our children to succeed and, for many people, the thought of what our kids do after high school is a big part of that. We don't want any of our choices along the way to interfere with their future.

The truth is:

- There is plenty of anecdotal evidence of homeschoolers being accepted to and graduating successfully from post-secondary education, both in the past and currently

- Many universities have homeschool specific admissions policies and are actively recruiting homeschoolers

- There are many ways to apply to post-secondary school, such as through an open university and transfer credits or as a mature applicant.

The key to success for your child's plans after high school is being proactive. No matter which path they decide to take, it is important to keep good records of what you've studied through the high school years to have a portfolio and transcript at the end. Communication with the school or program your child wants to attend will help you understand the expectations they have for accepting homeschooled students. Plus, you can try different options such as applying as a mature student, starting at an open university and transferring into another program after you have some credits in place, or even completing a General Educational Development test (GED) so you have some recognized paperwork if needed.

It's important to remember that university is only one of several options available to our kids after they finish high school. They can also go to community college, study a trade, get an apprenticeship, take a job, start a business, etc.

How your child approaches post-secondary options might not be the same path as their public schooled peers, but it's still a possibility.

DO WE HAVE TO DO TESTING?

Most provinces and territories don't require homeschooled children to complete or submit any level of testing - although that can change at any time with updates to regulations.

Standardized testing in schools is more to grade the school on their teaching as opposed to what the students know.

In the classroom setting, students take tests to evaluate what they have learned during a unit or subject. It allows a teacher to get a clearer picture of what each student knows or doesn't know.

Homeschoolers can do tests if they want as a way to review or confirm learning but, since you work closely with your children, you have a pretty clear understanding of what they know and don't know. We homeschoolers can teach for understanding, not for success with a test. Tests are only for your records and not for anything official to be submitted anywhere.

WHAT IF I'M NOT GOOD AT MATH/SPELLING/ETC.?

With such a wide variety of subjects over the years of schooling, there are going to be areas that you as a parent don't feel strong in or qualified to teach. The good news is that's okay. Even teachers at school aren't experts in everything. They use resources to help them put together lesson plans.

If you aren't feeling confident in one subject (or multiple subjects), use a curriculum that teaches it for you. One of the great things about homeschooling today is that we have resources available at our fingertips to reference as needed. There are tutors and programs and fantastic curriculum options we can outsource to.

Plus, there's a bonus to homeschooling. You get to learn right alongside your child, so you have a chance to figure out everything you've struggled with or didn't understand when you were a student!

YOUR ACTION STEP

If you still have any questions, write them down and look for the answers. There are many great voices in the homeschool blogging community, your local groups, and online support groups who can help answer them for you.

PART II:
LEARNING AND TEACHING

CHAPTER SIX

LEARNING STYLES

Before you dive headfirst into the (potentially bottomless) world of homeschooling curriculum and resources, I recommend you start by researching two things: your child's learning style and the various homeschooling methods. Choosing to consider these two areas first will help you narrow down your curriculum search and make it more personalized to your child's needs and your teaching preferences.

When you arrive at camp for the night, one of the first things you need to do is set up the tent. After dumping out the tent bag, how do you put it together?

Do you:

- look for the instructions and follow the pictures/text provided?

- have someone read them to you so you can follow the steps?

- grab all the pieces and just start putting it together, figuring it out as you go?

This answer has something to do with learning styles.

Learning styles are typically divided into 3 main options: visual, auditory, and kinesthetic.

Visual = seeing

Auditory = hearing

Kinesthetic = moving/doing

Although this is an oversimplification, it's generally a good place to start.

Children often tend to lean more into one of these styles, although it's not uncommon to have a combination. You will find you are better able to narrow down how your child best learns as your journey progresses. For now, it's a chance to use your observation skills and see how your children understand the world around them.

Have you noticed what your child does when learning something? Is there a way your child prefers to learn?

Here are some clues to look for.

Visual learners may:

- use picture clues in books to figure out what's happening
- be observant to details and changes
- take good notes and have neat handwriting
- have a hard time following verbal instructions
- doodle or enjoy art.

Auditory learners may:

- read books out loud to themselves (i.e., whispering the words)
- talk to themselves as they work on things

- want to discuss problems and solutions

- be easily distracted by sounds

- know all the words to songs.

Kinesthetic learners may:

- use their finger to follow along with the words in a book

- seem fidgety and wiggly when in a chair

- touch everything

- want to help with setting things up

- take things apart to figure out how they work.

When I look at my own life, I can see my learning style fairly quickly. Lots of people love podcasts and audiobooks. But if I put them on, my brain quickly wanders off into Lisa-land and I don't hear a thing. Auditory is not my learning style.

I am a combination of visual and kinesthetic learning. I have to actively engage myself in something in order to focus. For example, if I'm at a lecture or such, I have to take notes to keep my mind on the discussion. I never really studied for tests. Instead, I would think back to watching myself write notes during class.

How can you take what you've learned about your child's learning style and apply it to homeschooling?

If you have an idea how your children learn, you can make sure you include things that will help them understand more easily.

My children are all over the place. Many of them do best with visual learning, which means videos work great and read alouds do not. It means I've had to adapt some of the ways we do learning to make sure information is getting in.

If you have a visual learner, you can have them take notes. You can practice spelling with colours - for example, vowels are red and consonants are blue. Use checklists they can see for tasks that need to be done. Watch videos, especially on subjects they seem to be struggling with, so they can SEE how things work. Get models they can examine.

If you have an auditory learner, do read alouds. Get them to read things to you or to record their "notes" on a subject. Listen to educational pocasts. Give them verbal instructions. Discuss what they are learning together and allow them to do tests or presentations orally.

If you have a kinesthetic learner, prepare hands-on activities like science experiments. Tracing words on sandpaper is a great way to help them feel out how to spell words. Do physical activity while learning: jumping, clapping, and tapping, for example. Role playing can be fun. Use games and puzzles.

It's important to remember, even if your child seems to fall heavily into one of these common learning styles, that all areas of learning are vital. If we only focus on the one method where they learn best, they will be weak in the other areas.

Challenge your child to learn in ways that don't feel as easy. Teach them skills to be successful with other methods - like how I have to take active notes during anything that relies on listening to hear and understand.

Include all kinds of learning in your day.

As with everything covered in this book, remember that things change, adapt, and aren't set in stone. These are just tools we can use to make our teaching and learning experiences work better.

YOUR ACTION STEP

Spend some time watching your child and observe which learning style they naturally lean towards.

CHAPTER SEVEN

HOMESCHOOL METHODS

Choosing the perfect backpack for your travelling adventure is one of the biggest steps you take before getting started. There are so many options - features, sizes, colours, accessories. If you walk into an outfitter's shop and stand in their backpack section, there is a very good possibility you will be overwhelmed by the display of a hundred different packs.

Figure out which one is right for the adventure you are planning by:

- comparing features and picking the one that feels like it's the best option, and

- trying one on and testing it out.

It's the same thing with choosing a homeschool method. You may be wondering how exactly you are supposed to figure out which one will work for your family as you stand there looking at all the options.

#1. Compare and Pick

While looking at all the different options for homeschooling, take some time to look at the main features of each method. Some focus heavily on language. Some on nature studies. Others encourage the use of a child's curiosity. Some follow a strict plan and others are very relaxed. Looking over these ideals, consider which one has the most features that meet your preferences.

Which homeschool method feels like it's going to be the best fit for your family, your child, and your lifestyle? Pick that one.

#2. Test it Out

Pick one that seems good enough for now. You don't have to spend hours narrowing down your options and comparing the different features - just look at things in a brief overview and choose the one that looks the best.

Many homeschool families begin their journey with one homeschool style and adapt things as they become more comfortable with their journey. This is a natural ebb and flow kind of thing.

For example, a newly homeschooling family may start off doing school-at-home because it's as close to school as they can get, which offers a sense of security. In year two, they realize they love the idea of nature studies and add that into their days, along with reading aloud quality fiction books for history. In year three, they decide to change science from a textbook/workbook study to unit studies, where they dive in deep on a topic with hands-on activities, videos, and lapbooks.

By the end of year 3, they feel like they have settled into a great rhythm and mix of styles and resources that they are enjoying, pulling from traditional, Charlotte Mason, and unit studies. They've adapted into eclectic homeschoolers.

So, you can just pick one that feels right for now and give it a go.

Homeschooling offers the opportunity to approach learning and teaching differently than the traditional school system. There are lots of educational methodologies we can choose from — even mix and match from — to provide a very well rounded, thorough learning experience for our child.

Here are some of the main ones:

TRADITIONAL

A traditional or school-at-home approach is essentially trying to replicate the learning experience of a public school classroom at home: specific workspaces such as desks, textbooks and workbooks, assignments, and grades, often filling the day with structured study times and trying to match up to the same curriculum outlines set out by the government.

Many new homeschoolers (especially when they have had their child in the school system first) begin with the school-at-home approach since it is the most familiar to their own learning experience. There are two options for who teaches your child with this method: parent-led or teacher-led. Teacher-led programs are typically run as online academies or distance learning.

This method of homeschooling can include:

- a boxed curriculum set with textbooks and workbooks

- distance education / correspondence courses

- distributed learning

- online programs offered by an accredited online school or public school system

School-At-Home Benefits

- It's familiar because it follows a similar format and ideas of the common experience in school.

- It's easy to use. Many curricula in this method are laid out by day and are open and go.

- It's easy to buy since you can often get a whole grade of school resources in a single box.

- It's reassuring because you are sure your child is meeting all the expectations for their grade.

- It allows for easier transfer. If things change with your homeschooling adventure and you opt to put your child into school instead, you can feel pretty confident they are at par with their peers.

School-At-Home Disadvantages

- Purchasing a boxed curriculum for each grade tends to be quite expensive.

- Traditional learning doesn't account for differences in learning styles or preferences.

- It can require a lot of work each day from your child, which can lead to frustration and conflict.

- If you have unstable or limited internet, you might not be able to connect to online classes.

- It can put a lot of pressure and expectations on you as a parent/teacher, which can lead to burning out.

- It doesn't allow for flexibility of interest or schedules since you can have deadlines and a specific work schedule.

CLASSICAL

The Classical education method of homeschooling is based on the historical concept known as the trivium, which focuses on logic and reasoning as the centre of learning. This is broken up into three stages: Grammar, Logic, and Rhetoric, focusing on different skills as children grow and develop.

The Grammar stage is for the early years, up until around the end of elementary school grades. The focus is on the important building block foundations for future learning. Taking advantage of a child's natural ability to absorb information at this stage, many of the lessons focus on rote learning and memorization — such as spelling rules, mathematics facts, capital cities, etc. It's about repetition and learning facts.

Next is the Logic stage. This is when children are curious about why things happen and want to know more about cause and effect. It's a good time to learn the scientific method, how to critique things they read, and figure out why events happened in history. The logic stage focuses on the development of abstract thought.

High school is considered the Rhetoric stage — when students take what they've learned and apply it to life. It's about developing their own experience and opinions from what they've learned.

Classical education tends to lean heavily on languages, including root languages such as Greek and Latin, as well as classical literature, meaning reading and writing are a vital part of the learning.

Classical Education Benefits

- It gives a strong foundation in language skills.

- It encourages active mental learning.

- Classical education uses a child's natural mental developments and curiosities for learning.

- This method covers lots of classic literature.

Classical Education Disadvantages

- A heavy focus on reading can be challenging for struggling readers.

- This method can be parent intensive.

- Rote learning can be boring for some children.

CHARLOTTE MASON

Charlotte Mason was a British educator who lived around 1900. Her methodology of teaching focused on the whole child, not just academic facts.

This method is a parent-led approach that aims to fill a child with ideas as opposed to facts and data. Some of the key features of this method are:

- Nature Study — getting close to examine the natural world around them

- Outside Time — as much outside time as possible

- Living Books — quality fiction and non-fiction literature that bring subjects to life

- Habit Training — working on developing quality habits for everyday life

- Copywriting — handwriting of quality literature

- Short Lessons — allowing better focus and variety

One of her most popular quotes is, "Education is an atmosphere, a discipline, a life."

Charlotte Mason Benefits

- It focuses on the development of the whole child.

- Using living books helps children relate to what they are learning.

- It allows for lots of childhood free time and exploration of personal interests.

- Outside time and nature study are naturally built-in.

- It can be a very relaxed, child-centred learning experience.

Charlotte Mason Disadvantages

- A lot of reading is required, since this method uses books for every subject and topic.

- It can feel outdated since her methodology is from 100 years ago.

- Being outside in all weather may be a con for some — inclement weather can make for uncomfortable outside time.

- It can require a lot of parent-involvement, especially reading aloud.

- Books can be costly and take up a lot of room if you don't have library access or would rather buy them to keep.

UNSCHOOLING

Unschooling is a child-led homeschooling method that allows children to learn through life and curiosity. It's about finding answers and experiences for the questions they have at the moment, and discovering all they can learn about just from their everyday passions. It's about providing an atmosphere of exploration and inspiration.

Based on the ideals of a man named John Holt, the unschooling movement began officially in the 1970s. The goal of unschooling is to learn through life, such as moments experienced with interactions with others, the environment, their community, personal interests, their household, and volunteer opportunities.

Parents who unschool are facilitators more than typical teachers. They are actively involved in their children's learning, providing opportunities for them to explore, question, and discover naturally. They participate in their kids' interests and help them research answers to their questions.

Since the learning is guided by the child, unschoolers typically don't follow a curriculum or use workbooks but pull from a plethora of resources to find answers and dive into learning more.

Unschooling Benefits

- It's a relaxed and peaceful methodology.

- Since it's based on a child's natural interests, they are more likely to retain what they have learned.

- Kids discover that learning happens everywhere.

- It allows for mastery of personal interests.

- It is very family-centric, allowing for quality relationships with your children.

Unschooling Disadvantages

- Doing something opposite of social norms can be stressful.

- It can be hard to get past your own schooling experiences and allow complete freedom.

- It can be time-intensive as a parent to be involved, especially with multiple children.

- There can be gaps in what is considered "traditional learning expectations" — if that matters

- It can be harder to meet homeschool regulations with a complete unschooling approach in some provinces.

UNIT STUDIES

Unit studies are an all-encompassing, topic-focused approach that use resources for all subjects of a curriculum whenever possible to provide an in-depth learning experience. Often these studies start with a core resource book, then dig into extras, involve hands-on activities where possible, and expand through many subjects such as math, language, history, geography, etc.

A unit study approach involves creating a series of activities and learning experiences that all point back to a single generalized topic.

For example, a study on weather could include:

- creating weather instruments
- a field trip to a local weather station
- watching documentaries on storm chasers
- reading a historical fiction book about a weather-related event
- detailed journaling of weather records for each day
- comparing findings to the weather predictions
- comparing historical weather data to current details
- figuring out how to convert temperature from Fahrenheit to Celsius
- doing an experiment about the water cycle
- experimenting on how to create a cloud
- painting a picture of what their favourite weather looks like
- examining different weather patterns and learning how to predict weather with clues
- doing a craft that shows the different kinds of clouds
- watching the weather channel to follow the weather-related news
- volunteering to do a post-storm cleanup
- playing games on the computer.

The idea is to dive right into a topic and explore in as much detail as possible.

Many people enjoy using unit studies specifically for history and science. When doing it this way, the goal isn't to include all subjects but to focus more closely on a single subject.

Unit Study Benefits

- Great for families with multiple ages because everyone can be learning the same thing while adapting individual activities to various levels.

- It can focus on the interests of a child, making it more child-led.

- A wide selection of activities allows for different learning styles.

- Unit studies are particularly great for hands-on learners.

- They can be cost-efficient because you can use a variety of resources.

- They often can create long-term, positive memories of learning in your child.

- Many unit study lessons can be downloaded online and printed out instead of requiring large books.

Unit Study Disadvantages

- They can require a lot of planning and prep work for the parent.

- They have the potential to be quite messy from the hands-on activities.

- If your family has different age ranges, older children can feel like they are being held back in group learning times.

- You might need to supplement a unit study with additional content for other subjects like math.

MONTESSORI

The Montessori Method of homeschooling aims to follow the standards created by Dr. Maria Montessori in the early 1900s. She believed in creating an environment that encouraged self-directed learning opportunities through hands-on, play-based activities. This method focuses on experiences, rather than being taught.

Dr. Montessori set up a series of standards and expectations for students in her classes, such as:

- an environment of learning
- a whole room of activities that a child can pick from throughout the day, in whatever order they want
- a place where children can focus and concentrate on things they have chosen
- space for children to work independently and collaboratively
- encouraging independence and self-interest
- multi-aged classrooms
- allowing for younger students to learn from and imitate older students
- peer socialization
- quality, hands-on materials
- tactile and sensory-based
- child-sized
- limited access to technology
- self-correcting

- The Montessori curriculum focuses on 5 main areas: practical life skills, mathematics, sensory, language, and culture & science.

Montessori Benefits

- This method allows children to focus on independence.

- Children learn well because they are doing activities that interest them.

- It promotes a neat and tidy environment.

- The multi-age classroom idea works well for families with multiple children.

- It follows a child's skill level instead of a specific curriculum checklist.

Montessori Disadvantages

- It involves a lot of parental planning and prep to set up centres.

- It's specifically designed for younger children, such as preschool and early elementary, and may not be able to be used at higher ages as easily.

- This approach is more intentional and doesn't allow for much imaginative play.

- Manipulatives can be quite costly.

WALDORF

The Waldorf method of homeschooling was created by an Austrian man named Rudolf Steiner in 1919 when he opened his first school. He believed education should be inclusive of the whole child (head, heart, and hands) while focusing heavily on the arts, folklore and mythology, and the natural world.

In a Waldorf curriculum, reading is delayed until later in the 2nd grade, focusing on oral stories and understanding of letters and writing first. The arts are interwoven with all other subjects to make them more tangible and beautiful.

In a classroom model, especially in the early years, students often have the same teacher for several years. This is designed to create a family-like atmosphere for learning.

There are also some unique features included in their education such as eurythmy (movement with language), inclusion of handiwork such as knitting, an early introduction to world languages, and a single intentional block of time each day (between 1 – 2 hours) set aside for teaching/learning.

Many of the toys and resources are made from natural materials such as woods, silks, and beeswax. There is a general avoidance of technology and television.

In the early years, an emphasis is placed on imagination, storytelling, and developing an appreciation for the beauty of the arts and world around them. In the older grades, art skills are refined as students turn the things they've learned in various subjects into beautiful textbooks. High school is where students are believed to fully grasp more abstract thoughts and learning.

Waldorf Benefits

- The combination of academics with the arts makes learning memorable.

- This method encourages looking at things from different approaches, leading to an ability to think outside the box.

- A vivid imagination is encouraged.

- It uses a co-operative approach to learning, rather than competitive.

- All areas of learning are considered as equally important as others.

Waldorf Disadvantages

- Steiner himself believed in a faith called anthroposophy which has to do with awareness of a spiritual self. Despite attempting to create an education model that focuses on a child's natural wonder at creation, some of the basic roots of his belief systems are integrated into everyday learning. Some find the religious basis for the program concerning.

- Delayed academics can be of concern for some (but this can also be a benefit for others).

- It can be expensive to get quality materials.

- A heavy emphasis on the arts might not be a good fit for all children.

- Families favouring technology might find the non-tech approach challenging.

RELAXED / MINIMALIST

Relaxed or minimalist homeschooling follows the popular movement to simply one's life by only keeping the things that matter most. In this method, learning is pared down to the most important things with lots of space and free time for additional exploration. It's a cross-breed of unschooling mashed with formal learning — although the approach to the basic subjects may be done using any method.

It can also be about removing all the "things" we collect as homeschoolers — the mountain of books, the hoard of art supplies, the paper piles, etc. In truth, it's more about simplification and the removal of what we don't need. It's about changing our mindset to not be like everyone else but to focus on the things that are most valuable to us.

Curricula is generally a mixed and matched collection instead of a specific program. It's about personalization.

Relaxed / Minimalist Homeschooling Benefits

- This method is very personalized to the needs of the children.
- It's a relaxed approach with less stress than some other homeschool methods.
- It works well with a large family.
- It allows for a lot of free time.

Relaxed Homeschooling Disadvantages

- Since it focuses on only what the family deems important, subject gaps may exist.

62

- It can take a while to settle into a rhythm that works for your family.

- It may involve a lot of group learning, which might not work with your family dynamics.

- It involves a mindset change to allow that less is more, which can be challenging.

ECLECTIC

Eclectic homeschooling is like a patchwork quilt — a little bit of this, a little bit of that. It is a mishmash of any style of homeschooling and curriculum that works for your family.

Families often end up landing in the eclectic style once they settle into a homeschooling rhythm. Picking and choosing resources makes your homeschooling experience individualized to your child's needs and your family dynamics. It allows you to use parts of other methods that appeal to you and make it your own learning experience.

Sometimes homeschooling methods are compared to a buffet table. One style of homeschooling might be able to only eat from this part of the table. Another from the other end. One might be heavy on desserts while the other shuns sweets altogether. Eclectic homeschoolers can eat from everything and anything as they want. There are no rigid rules to follow or expectations to hold, just the freedom to take what works and leave the rest.

Eclectic Benefits

- You can pick the best resources using the best method for your child, family, and subject.

- You aren't confined to a set of rules.

- It's extremely flexible and adaptable.

- It can be quite cost-effective as you only buy what you feel you need.

Eclectic Disadvantages

- There are so many curriculum options available within all the homeschooling methods that it can be overwhelming.

- New homeschoolers may find the idea of using multiple methods overwhelming because it doesn't have any specific guidelines.

- It can require a lot of time on the parent's behalf to figure out the perfect fit per child or subject.

YOUR ACTION STEP

Figure out which homeschool method feels like the best fit for you, your child, and your family.

PART III:
ABOUT CURRICULUM

CHAPTER EIGHT

HOW MUCH DOES HOMESCHOOLING COST?

One of the first questions considered when someone is researching homeschool is "How much does homeschooling cost?" The answer isn't an easy one because it involves many elements.

Homeschooling costs vary extremely, depending on what method you use, which resources you choose, how much work you can or want to do as a parent/teacher, and what extras you include. It can be easy to rack up expenses, but you can also homeschool on a very small budget. Costs can range from practically free to extremely expensive.

Things that might cost money when you are homeschooling include:

- curricula

- technology tools like computers, e-readers, tablets, and printers

- equipment like a microscope, whiteboard or blackboard, etc.

- consumables such supplies for art projects and science experiments

- school supplies and furniture

- books
- memberships to museums, galleries, a gym, and other learning centres
- extra-curricular fees
- field trips
- subscriptions to online programs
- transportation costs

One of the great things about homeschooling is that you have options. You are not obligated to get or use or do anything specific — you can decide what is within the budget you have and work with that. The bigger your available budget, the more options you have, but it's not required.

If you buy a complete boxed-set curriculum from a publisher, you will generally find this to be the most expensive option. Costs of some popular programs range anywhere from $350 per grade to over $1000. The trade-off, however, is that you will typically be able to open your books and get started with minimal prep, knowing you have everything all together for the year.

Many homeschool families decide to mix and match their curriculum instead of buying an all-in-one set. This not only allows for a more individualized plan but can often save money.

Many people are curious if you can homeschool for free. The answer is yes, but it usually comes with a different expense — typically time, effort, and printing.

There have been times in our homeschooling journey where our family lived under the poverty line and struggled to put food on the table. During these years, there was no extra money to spend on homeschooling resources. It was simply impossible. Instead, I spent countless hours and days putting together plans with resources I found for free or very cheap.

To homeschool for free, you typically have to piece together a plan — creating or finding resources and activities to match your goals for the year. Thanks to sites like Pinterest, YouTube, and TeachersPayTeachers, we have so many more options and resources than homeschoolers ever had before. However, it can be labour intensive to make your own curriculum plans each year.

It can also be easy to think you are doing it for free only to realize there is a huge cost involved with printing a large collection of printables. My advice is to spend the money on a quality printer that will save you on ink in the long run. Cheap printers are great — until you see how often you have to refill the ink cartridges! Buy a good one on sale. Watch for great discounts during the back to school season.

There are a few complete online programs that allow you to homeschool for free, since the creators have already gone through the work of piecing it together for you. The downside to these free programs can be that they might not match your child's learning style or your preferred homeschooling method. Some of them can feel quite antiquated since they use old resources and books. However, the only costs to you are the books needed, your internet fees, and printing any worksheets. Some examples of this are:

- Easy Peasy All-in-One Homeschool

- Ambleside Online

- An Old-Fashioned Education

Some free programs focus on specific subjects only, so you can combine them to make a full program of your own. Plus, there are tons of free individual lesson plans available online for just about any topic you are looking to study. You just have to find them and prepare them for use.

HOW TO SAVE MONEY ON HOMESCHOOLING (ESPECIALLY AS A CANADIAN)

One challenge of being a homeschooler in Canada is that many of the resources we want to use are published by companies in the US. That means we have to deal with the added expenses of the exchange rate and a high cost of shipping. Even within Canada, shipping can be costly. Here are some ways you can save money on curriculum.

- Buy used. Look for the books and resources you'd like to buy on swap groups, curriculum sales, thrift stores, friends, sites like eBay and Kijiji, etc. However, not all programs are legally allowed to be resold, so be sure to respect publishers and follow their copyright rules.

- Buy digital. Some publishers offer digital editions of their resources, which means huge savings in shipping costs. Plus you can use it again with another child, if applicable. Of course, this also means you might need to print things out. Try reading the files and having your child answer worksheets on your computer or tablet instead of printing the whole thing out (or use a spiral notebook to answer questions separately.)

- Reuse. If you have multiple children at different stages, intentionally buy resources you can reuse. Spending more money on a program you love for child #1 but never have to buy again for subsequent children can save you astronomical amounts of money.

- Resell. If you are done with a resource and know you don't need to use it again — sell it. Please make sure you are allowed under the rules of the publisher before you do so. This can get money back into your pocket to buy something else.

- Wait for sales. Homeschool curriculum publishers often put their resources on sale in the spring (conference season) and mid-summer when people realize they need books to start lessons in the fall. Keep your eye open for discounts and free shipping offers.

- Ship it to a US mailbox. Many Canadians save on shipping by getting their curriculum sent to a friend or family member in the US or to a mailbox they rent across the border. Then they take a trip to the States to pick the order up. Of course, this tip only works if you live close enough to the border to do so.

- Buy local. Look for a Canadian distributor or store close to you and buy from them. Sometimes you can even pick up in person to save shipping costs altogether.

- Buy with friends. If you know other local homeschoolers using the same curriculum or buying from the same store, place a group order and split the costs of shipping. This can be a great way to lower your overall shipping expenses.

- Shop around. Often, there are better deals for curricula on non-publisher websites. Check different stores and compare the prices and shipping and the cost of the exchange rate versus buying from a store in Canada.

- Don't feel pressured to buy expensive. You do NOT have to buy a boxed curriculum or the most popular names in the homeschooling community — you can buy or use more cost-efficient resources that are a good fit for your family. Just because it seems like everyone else is using a particular curriculum, doesn't mean you need to spend the large amounts of money it can often cost.

In summary, the question "How much does homeschooling cost?" is dependent on how you homeschool, what resources you use, and how many of the money-saving tips you put into practice while homeschooling.

A family can homeschool for free when a parent is willing to put time and effort into pulling together resources to make their plans. However, for some, the freedom offered by an open and go curriculum is worth every penny.

The main question probably shouldn't be "How much does homeschooling cost?" but more "What can we afford to spend on our homeschool resources?" and then choosing things that fit within that budget.

YOUR ACTION STEP

Figure out what you can or want to budget for homeschool resources and activities this year.

CHAPTER NINE

THE PRESCHOOL YEARS

Around the ages of 3 or 4, parents start to feel pressured about academics for their child. That sense of urgency prompts them to search for curriculum because that seems like the most obvious way to replicate school at home. However, formal learning isn't needed for a child who is 3 or 4.

There are five keys to learning in the early years: Play. Read. Live. Connect. Create.

KEY #1: PLAY

Learning through play is the single most important thing in early childhood education.

Mr Rogers said it best,

"Play is often talked about as if it were a relief from serious learning, but for children play is serious learning. Play is really the work of childhood."

Creating opportunities for your child to learn through play is a vital key to their development. But what does this look like?

There are two basic forms of play: free play and guided/directed play.

Free play is where kids go and do their own thing without a grown-up or outside influence. They aren't told how to play - they just do it.

What kind of learning opportunities can free play offer? One really important thing is discovering their abilities and limits. During free play, kids often challenge themselves. They discover what they can and cannot do.

Have you ever seen a child play uninterrupted in the sandbox? They are learning all kinds of things: gravity, properties of matter, how adding water can change the consistency of sand, and the ability of sand to be molded. They learn about dirty and clean. They develop fine motor skills and gross motor skills. They are natural-born scientists, and they don't even know it.

Watch your little one for a day as they putter around, exploring their world, interacting with things or people. Every moment is a learning experience or opportunity. When they build towers with blocks, they are discovering attributes of shapes (rectangles have long sides so you can stack things on top of them, but if you put a cylinder on its side, it rolls away). When they build it too high, they learn objects fall over because they get too unstable. When they play on the playground, they learn stairs make it easy to get up to the top. When they talk to other kids, they have to learn how to communicate effectively, how to share, how to take turns, etc. When they run up the slide at the playground, they learn their limits as well as pushing their gross motor (big muscle) skills.

Directed play is when an adult sets the boundaries for play through things like dramatic centres or board games, for example. Typically, directed play has intentional learning objectives. We want to guide their learning to something specific.

For example, we might set up a grocery store dramatic play centre in our house. While our children can use it to play naturally, we control the basic learning expectations within this experience. It intentionally teaches:

- money concepts
- food groups
- sorting and organizing
- community helpers
- conventional social skills

You can create simple resources or opportunities to learn. One of my personal favourites for the little guys is something we call "noodle math." Give your child a pile of dry noodles and on a piece of paper, draw some circles. Write a number in each circle and ask your child to put the right amount of noodles in each circle. It's a game they love to play. You can create file folder games or busy bags which allow kids to explore a single skill on their own. You can write letters on index cards and lay them out all over the floor to hop on, calling out letter names or sounds as they land on a card.

As a parent, you just need to offer them the tools to play and the space to explore. This doesn't have to be expensive. It can be as simple as a magnifying glass and a bin of leaves. Or a stick, sand, and water. It can also be a bin of LEGO pieces, a simple game like memory, or a collection of musical instruments.

The thought here is to create play-centred activities that allow your child to learn something, whether intentionally or incidentally. When learning is fun, kids retain more, understand more, and want to know more.

A key aspect of this is also communication. Ask questions, think out loud to your child in a way that gets them explaining their thoughts in return, and make observations on things. Get them talking and interacting while they play.

KEY #2: READ

Author Emilie Buchwald once said, "Children are made readers on the laps of their parents." It's true. If we introduce them to the world of books, role model reading, and give them time to read with us, kids will love books — at least while they are young.

Reading inspires imagination, engages the creativity children naturally have, affords opportunities for expanded learning, and helps develop early language skills. Pick books that are full of great pictures and language. Talk about what you see in those pictures. Use your finger to follow along with the words on the second time through. If you use books with repetitive language, pause to let your child fill in the blanks.

KEY #3: LIVE

Modelling life skills and encouraging the involvement of our children in everyday life is a wonderful tool for preschool learning time. Little children tend to follow a parent around, wanting to do whatever the grown-up is doing. This is a perfect opportunity to encourage hands-on learning.

- They can help sort laundry, move it from machine to machine, and fold it when it's done.

- They can help in the kitchen with cooking and baking, and learning how to clean up when it's finished.

- They can do chores around the house like dusting, sweeping and mopping the floors, and wiping down counters.

- They can set the table and unload the dishwasher.

- They can bring in the recycling box, turn on the sprinkler, and water the plants.

Give them opportunities to do house repairs. Let them learn how to use basic tools like hammers and screwdrivers.

Kids are fascinated by the everyday things in their lives. Use that as a chance to encourage their participation.

KEY #4: CONNECT

Use the resources and community around you to provide learning experiences and chances to interact with others. Kids need to learn how to connect not only with peers but also with a wide age range of people from babies to elders. Here are some easy ways to do that:

- Go to the library. Not only can you get access to a plethora of interesting and fun reading materials, but libraries also offer programs for all ages. I've seen preschool storytime, LEGO club, Make & Take craft days, and even science exploring.

- Go to the playground. Any playground. Then let them run wild. Kids will more often than not gravitate to other kids to share their most important details like "I'm 4" instead of their names.

Then they play like best friends until parents drag them away. This is free, fun, and full of exercise while offering opportunities to connect with kids of all ages.

- Go to a senior's care centre. Elderly people love little kids. It can be a total bright spot in an otherwise quiet day. See if there is a nursing home or community centre near you that offers times for visitors with children to come and hang out.

- Find free / cheap activities in the community. See if stores like Home Depot offer kids' workshops. Some art galleries have free family art days where you can go and art your heart out. Check the community listings — sometimes cities have events like history days, concerts, or fairs you can take your kids to. There are farmers' markets you can visit as well.

- Look for homeschool groups near you. Lots of times homeschoolers have community groups you can join in for field trips, playdates, and other activities. It's worth connecting with other homeschooling families so you can grow together and create a network of fun and friends.

KEY #5: CREATE

Give your child the chance to use their inner artist. As Pablo Picasso said, "Every child is an artist."

Some easy ways to encourage art are to have a junk box full of miscellaneous things such as empty toilet paper rolls, cotton balls, elastics, string, pieces of wrapping paper or fabric, Popsicle sticks, pipe cleaners, etc. Give them access to tape and glue and watch them create.

Have time to pull out the paint and markers.

If the thought of mess makes you anxious, some great tips are to use the No Mess markers from Crayola that only work on a specific type of paper. You can use a whiteboard for art time - which contains it to a smaller space. You can set up an easel outside so paint doesn't get all over the house. You can use water to "paint."

The idea is to let your little one explore art and ignite that creative side of themselves.

TECHNOLOGY FOR PRESCHOOL

Kids love computers and games. If you are okay with intentional learning through technology, use that to your advantage and provide some learning opportunities through the digital medium.

- Starfall.com — This website (and app) has both a free and membership section. The free section includes some quality language resources, starting with letters and sounds and moving to more difficult skills like putting sounds together to make words and eventually even stories. There are also some interactive activities and games like building a gingerbread man, adding faces to pumpkins, etc. Membership content is more in-depth, adding math and higher-level learning resources. The animations on this site are fun and little kids enjoy the bright colours combined with silliness. This site is a great way to teach mouse skills as well because whenever something needs to be clicked, it sparkles. There are also printables you can download and books you can buy.

- Teach Your Monster to Read — In this game, your child has their own monster and has to do mini-games to earn prizes and gear and such. These games focus on phonics and words, progressively getting more challenging the farther along they get. It's available as a website and also as an app.

- ABCya.com — This site has games for kids from Pre-K right through Grade 6+, all carefully sectioned by level and by subject. There are lots of options for games to play.

- Reading Eggs / MathSeeds — This site has two sections: one for reading and one for math. On both sections, your child has a character they use to navigate through a map. Each stop on the map involves a series of games and activities to develop math or number skills. There are many maps and levels, allowing your child to continue to work through the game until they are much older. They get to buy things for their character with rewards they earn for completing activities.

- Originator Apps — This is a series of fantastic apps. Our favourite is Endless ABC where you drag the letters around the screen to put them in place and they make their phonetic sound while you move them. It's really fun, entertaining, and educational.

USING A PRESCHOOL CURRICULUM

When you set your 3- or 4-year-old down with a workbook and expect them to finish a page of math, you run the risk of creating an association between school and boredom or frustration. That's not going to encourage them to want to do school at any point. Once you've killed their natural interest in learning, it can be incredibly hard to get it back.

Does this mean you should never allow your child a workbook or intentional academics? No. For your little ones, having some simple workbooks available can be fun. You can encourage them to try it out, or let them tell you they want to use workbooks. But don't FORCE them to do it. Make it casual, fun, and interesting. Let them decide when they are done or even what pages they want to work on. They can build up to intentional, structured "school" time when they are older.

If you just want something to give you a guideline on what to do each day, try to choose a curriculum that is not going to be heavy and demanding on your little one. These early years aren't about forcing your child to learn how to read or master addition. It's about creating a foundation for learning. Here are a few examples of play-based learning programs:

- Five in a Row / Come Sit By Me — These programs both use children's picture books as their theme. Basically, for a week, you read a central book and do activities that connect with it. Come Sit By Me is Canadian and focuses on Canadian picture books, where Five in a Row uses all sorts of stories.

- LetteroftheWeek.com — This program creates a foundation of reading skills, starting with letters and moving to sounds and stories as your child gets older. It includes a recommended weekly schedule with activities that reinforce the letter or sound of the week through a wide variety of subjects.

A DIY PRESCHOOL PLAN

If you search for "preschool curriculum" you will notice a trend. Many preschool programs are run based on themes, such as seasons or holidays, topics of interest, picture books or stories, or letters or numbers. Having a theme makes early learning easy. Picking a single topic and connecting all the outside pieces to it means you get immersed in that subject until you move onto the next. (This is actually what the unit study homeschooling methodology is like — picking a topic and connecting all other subjects to it.)

For example, let's say your theme is The Very Hungry Caterpillar by Eric Carle. Here are some ways to connect your learning to that story.

1. Create a food station with cut out pictures of different foods to sort into basic food groups (health).

2. Have a food tasting day where you try foods the caterpillar ate (science).

3. Learn about the metamorphosis life cycle of a butterfly with a simple craft (art & science).

4. Make fingerprint caterpillars with a different number of body segments (math).

5. Get a butterfly kit and grow a caterpillar into a butterfly (science).

6. Hunt for caterpillars and butterflies outside (nature & science).

7. Make a caterpillar out of egg cartons (art).

8. Move your body like a caterpillar, curl up like a cocoon, fly like a butterfly, etc. (physical education).

9. Make cards with all the foods the caterpillar ate and get kids to make matching groups and count (math).

Preschoolers are like sponges. They absorb so much information and learning through everyday life. It can be tempting to use this time to fill up your day with workbooks and seatwork — but don't forget to enjoy these early days by following the wisdom of the Magic School Bus teacher, Ms Frizzle: "Take Chances, Make Mistakes, Get Messy!"

The most important thing? This is not a race.

While yes, some little learners pick up reading faster than other kids or excel in math or other areas of academics, your goal isn't to get your preschooler to first place. It's to enjoy the time together and to help nurture a life of curious and passionate learning. It's about appreciating the wonder of childhood innocence while you can. They don't have to be reading by the time they are 6 — you won't be setting them up for failure.

Play. Read. Live. Connect. Create. That's all that you need to do.

CHAPTER TEN
THE HIGH SCHOOL YEARS

Preparing to start homeschooling through high school can easily have this overwhelming and sudden sense of pressure. However, it doesn't have to be stressful. You just have to come up with a plan that works for you and your child.

STEP #1: DIPLOMA OR NO DIPLOMA

The very first decision you have to make is if you are going to work towards an "official government-issued diploma" or not. This is completely dependent on your child's goals and plans and what works for your family. There are plenty of options here.

- Take accredited courses through correspondence or online programs.

- Do your own thing completely. Keep well-documented notes of programs and courses you do at home to issue your own homeschool graduation diploma.

- A combination of the two, depending on what is available and offered in your province/territory. There may be options to write challenge exams or to get the curriculum you've used independently at home converted into official credits. Do some research to see if any of these are options you can consider.

Pros of Getting a Diploma

- Getting a government-issued diploma might make post-secondary applications easier.

- It's universally recognized.

Cons of Getting a Diploma as a Homeschooler

- You usually have to complete courses from accredited programs, which might not work to your method, delivery preference, or worldview.

- You may need to take extra steps for qualification, such as SAT or literacy tests.

Pros to Doing Your Own Thing

- You can study in a method that works for you with the curriculum and subject areas you choose.

Cons to Doing Your Own Thing

- You might need to jump through more hoops for post-secondary applications.
- It may not be recognized as a diploma in some situations.

STEP #2: MAKE A PLAN

Once you've decided whether you will work towards a government diploma or not, the next step is figuring out what you will learn over the next four years. With help from your student, decide what subjects you want to study each year so you have a complete path.

Even if you choose to do your own thing through high school, using the government expectations for graduation can give you a good starting place for what courses to include during the high school years.

Typically, high school requires a series of courses in core subjects: language arts, math, science, history/geography, the arts, a second language, physical education and health, and career studies. Outside of that, additional credits are needed. There are called electives and allow for personal interest in a variety of topics. Electives can include things like work co-ops, religious studies, computer programming, business, a foreign language, auto mechanics, or even courses done as dual-credit at a local college or university.

A complete credit is usually considered to be 110-120 hours of work.

Pencil in a basic outline so you know what topics you are doing when. Then you are ready to move onto the next step.

STEP #3: PICK A PROGRAM

Once you know which topics you want to cover during high school, it's time to figure out what curriculum or program you are going to use.

We will cover how to search for a homeschool curriculum in the next section of this book.

STEP #4: ADD VOLUNTEERING / EXTRAS

Whether you are working towards getting a diploma or not, providing teenagers with opportunities to volunteer and help in the community is a good idea. It helps them think of others and get out in the world. Search for volunteer opportunities at local churches, community centres, kids' clubs, homeschool groups, retirement homes, and regional websites.

The Duke of Edinburgh Award is a program for high school students to work on achieving goals and challenges in service, skills, physical activity, and adventure. It gets students active in their communities and exploring their interests. Find out more at www.dukeofed.org.

STEP #5: KEEP RECORDS

Write down everything — the title of the resources and curriculum you use, books you read, topics and units covered, activities done, how you determined grades, the grades themselves, etc. to be able to put together a detailed transcript and course descriptions, if needed.

The best advice I've heard about homeschooling through high school is from veteran homeschool mom Louise House from The Learning House (learninghouse.ca): "The most important word, in my mind, is the word 'proactive'."

She advises being proactive when considering what courses your student should take. If your child is likely to head into a university program, make sure from the beginning that you have academically challenging courses that will be good preparation. If not, choosing less strenuous courses will make your student's high school years more enjoyable.

Her other advice is to be proactive in planning for post-secondary admissions. If your student knows what they would like to do after high school, you should start contacting prospective post-secondary schools. Look at the college/university website for their pre-requisites for the program you are considering. Connect with the administration's office to ask what they require of a homeschooled student, especially if your child won't have a government-issued high school diploma. Each school has its own way of doing things.

Plus, it is important to call regularly to make sure everything that is required and submitted is actually in your student's file for review when you apply.

Although at first homeschooling through high school can seem overwhelming, once you have a plan, you can breathe easy knowing every step is in place.

CHAPTER ELEVEN

CHOOSING CURRICULUM

So far in this book, you've figured out why you are homeschooling, observed your children to see how they learn, and considered which homeschooling method will work best for your family. Now it's time to take what you've learned and figure out what you are going to use.

Choosing curricula is the one step that tends to overwhelm, panic, and stress people out. It can be one of the hardest steps to take while homeschool planning. Let's face it — there are SO many choices out there. There can be too many choices. My advice: do not just search "homeschool curriculum" online because you will get millions and millions of results. This is why you spent time doing the last two steps. Knowing WHAT you want to teach and HOW you want to teach it helps narrow down those options.

The first real step to getting started with planning your homeschool year is to put together a general overview of what you are going to teach and learn throughout the year. This could be as basic as what actual academic subjects you are going to teach (math, science, history, etc.), what topics you would like to learn through a unit study (like horses, space, or dinosaurs), or it could be more ideas for specific targeted goals like "able to write in cursive" or "memorize all times tables to 12×12."

Make sure your goals are developmentally appropriate and personalized to your child. Remember, this step is just about figuring out what your goals are for the year and/or what subjects you want to cover. Don't over complicate things.

QUESTIONS TO ASK

Because there are so many options, a good place to start is answering a few more questions to narrow down your own personal preferences.

- Do you need or want to follow the government outlines for your province or territory?

- Do you care if the curriculum is faith-based or not?

- Do you care if the curriculum has Canadian content?

- Do you want a program that is open & go with daily plans of exactly what you are to do or do you want more flexibility?

- Are you okay with online or technology-based resources or would you prefer offline?

- Do you want to do group learning or independent learning if you have multiple children?

Is there anything else you consider a must in your homeschool curriculum or plans?

A note here: You will find that the homeschool market is saturated with Christian American resources. If you want something Canadian, prepare to mix and match because there currently isn't a boxed set for Canadians. Also, there are some great secular resources out there, but again — you might need to search a little deeper to find what you want.

ACTION STEP

Take some time to answer these questions and think about what is important for you to have in a curriculum.

CHAPTER TWELVE

THE SEARCH FOR CURRICULUM

Once you have all the questions answered and situations considered, if you've decided to use a curriculum, it's time to look for the materials for this year.

Don't just dive right in and ask a general "What curriculum should I use for Grade 2?" in a Facebook group or start searching through Google. You will get millions and millions of answers - and the overwhelm is very likely to hit hard. Instead, we're going to use what you know to get specifically what you need.

Start with one subject per kid at a time while searching so you don't get overwhelmed. Instead of being general, try to search exactly what you are looking for. Of course, this might not always work as not every combination is going to have a resource for it, but it's a good place to start. For example, you can search "Homeschool math hands-on Charlotte Mason" and see what comes up as suggestions. Get as detailed in your search as possible. Don't just check Google — look at other resources, too.

Reading reviews of products is a great way to get feedback on what works and what doesn't for different homeschooling families. See if there are any curriculum samples on company websites that you can download or try. Read the testimonials on their site, look through Pinterest, search for homeschooling blog reviews, see if there are any YouTube videos of people using the product.

If you can go to a homeschool conference, take the opportunity to meet the vendors, check out their materials, and chat with other homeschoolers about what they like and don't like.

Consider the price, the resell/reuse factor, and how much planning & prep work you as the teacher will need to do.

Don't be afraid to be creative either. There are a lot of amazing online classes and programs, digital and printable resources, and other unique options to choose from.

When you find a possible fit, write it down on your page. If you find multiple options, write them down to compare. Pick something that sounds like it will work and move onto the next subject or child until complete.

When you've finally got everything picked out and planned, you need to buy what you need. Check out used curriculum sales first (but make sure you are only buying resources that are allowed to be resold). Facebook is a great place for this. Look for local and provincial swap groups. There is also a Canada-wide group.

If you can't find it for resale, keep an eye out for sales at stores and with publishers. The most common time for resources to be on sale is between April and September. If you like digital products, watch for homeschool digital bundle sales in that same time frame.

IF YOU WANT TO DO UNIT STUDIES

Planning to learn through unit studies involves a few different steps than some other methods.

Often these studies start with a main resource book, dig into extras, involve hands-on activities where possible, and expand through many subjects such as math, language, history, geography, etc. Usually, this method involves getting very comfortable with your local library, your computer, and the related resources that might be available in your community. Popular ways to showcase what you've learned are through compiled presentation methods such as lapbooks, notebooks, or scrapbooks, but more technological options such as videos and blogging are available, too.

If this is the way you want to teach your kids, how can you get started learning like this?

Option 1: Find or buy pre-made / pre-prepared unit studies.

One of the wonderful things about our world today is that you can find just about anything you want online. There are quite a few terrific unit study resources available out there on just about any topic! Just search for your topic + "unit study" to see what comes up.

Option 2: Create Your Own.

Making your own unit studies can be a lot of fun, and allows you to tailor-fit them to your child's favourite subjects and interests.

First, pick a topic to study and figure out how long you want to study it for. Break down the main topic into small subtopics to make dividing it up into lessons easier. A good secret to doing this is by looking at the table of contents of textbooks or the navigation headers of websites on the topic you want to study.

For example, if you are studying Ancient Egypt, you might break it down into topics like:

- geography of Egypt
- historical periods (Old Kingdom, Middle Kingdom, New Kingdom)
- pharaohs
- mummification and pyramids

Next, collect a selection of ideas to help study this topic.

Look for books, videos, websites, field trips, games and interactive activities, resources in the community, people you can have as guests or visitors to teach, crafts and/or hands-on projects to do, etc. The goal is to saturate your child's learning experience with a fun, creative, memorable, and educational focus on the topic of choice.

When you have a list of all sorts of resources and ideas, separate them into their subtopics and fill in your time frame. If you have a lot of things for one subtopic, or that subtopic has a lot of information to learn, you will probably want to spend more time on it. Sort your resources into what you think you can reasonably accomplish in a day and/or how long you want to study it for.

Then you are all set to go!

THE BEST LAID PLANS

Remember, this step is going to take time. It's not always easy to figure out exactly what will be right for your child and your homeschooling adventures. And even if you think you've found something amazing... it might be a total flop.

Many homeschoolers discover that their carefully weighed plans haven't worked out. Please know it's okay to drop or change something in the middle of a year. Even if it seemed perfect, if it's not working and can't be adapted to work, it's perfectly acceptable to switch to another plan. Homeschooling is about flexibility and personalizing your learning experience. Don't feel trapped by the curriculum you choose.

Curriculum is honestly a trial-and-error adventure with your kids. All you can do is choose what you think is going to work best and then test it out.

YOUR ACTION STEP

Spend some time considering your curriculum options using all the pieces you've put together so far. Figure out what you will use this year — if you have decided to use curriculum.

CHAPTER THIRTEEN
THE CANADIAN PORTION

Many Canadians choose to use American-based curriculum materials in their homeschool for a wide variety of reasons. However, there can sometimes be challenges surrounding the use of American materials as the content isn't always relevant to our life experiences or are missing things we want to be sure to include, such as history or geography.

If you are using a US curriculum, and are wondering how to adapt it to fit your family here in Canada, here are a few suggestions:

Look for a Canadian supplement or edition of your curriculum materials.

See whether the curriculum you want to use has a Canadian version, or if the company itself has provided a Canadian supplement or information on how to adapt their materials. Sometimes other homeschooling parents have put the time and work into making and providing curriculum changes to help their fellow homeschoolers.

Cover it up with Canadian materials.

For example, when learning about coins and money, take Canadian coins and physically cover up the drawings of the US coins. Or use stickers. Cross out words spelled American style and write them in Canadian spelling instead.

Parallel the Content.

If there are things in your curriculum that are explicitly American and you want to make sure your child knows the Canadian perspective on that topic, create parallel content. When studying history, for example, create a parallel timeline with Canadian history that goes along with it. Merge the two topics. Use the opportunity to compare and contrast.

Substitute.

If there are units of study in your curriculum you don't think are relevant to your child's education as a Canadian (or would be better used to provide Canadian content instead), just skip that section and grab an additional unit from somewhere else to substitute in its place.

A good example could be a unit on geography; maybe you'd like to teach your child about the geography of Canada instead of the US. During that segment, use a Canadian geography program instead.

Just go with it.

And finally, if you've chosen to use an American curriculum, you can just go with what it teaches. There's no obligation or requirement to add in, replace, or include Canadian content in your homeschooling adventures. Teach your child the richness of American history, the vastness of their geography, and all the other small differences between our two cultures without guilt. Learning is learning!

CANADIAN HISTORY

Canadian history seems to be the one area homeschoolers in Canada struggle with. We are all trying to figure out the best way to get this information into our kids without making it boring, whitewashed, or overwhelming.

If I was to ask you to give me a moment of history that was amazing or interesting or exciting, what would you say? Chances are it wouldn't be something that happened in Canadian history. That's because, for many people, Canadian history is considered boring. There are some good reasons for that — such how it is often presented in school as just a series of dates and facts or that we don't have any large flash-bang! moments.

Canadian history is much more subtle. Instead of being able to ramble off events on a timeline, our history needs to be taught in a much more personal way.

On the big timeline of history, Canada's recorded history is quite short. It doesn't have any major events or special features that draw attention to it on a grand scale, so it's easy to figure it isn't fun or important. To study Canadian history and make it more exciting, we need to zoom in closely and narrow our focus onto the people and specific moments of our story.

As with all things we teach our children, it's important to find ways to make the subject understandable, engaging, and maybe a little exciting. History is no different and, although our own experiences are often lacking, there are a lot of fun ways to enjoy teaching Canadian history.

- Get closer to the action than a wide overview. Realizing we don't have the same monumental events and long history to draw from, we need to zoom in on the moments, places, and people of specific parts of our story. Get closer to the action than a wide overview.

- Role model interest and engagement to our kids. Be excited and inspire curiosity.

- Learn about people. Kids want to know about the people who experienced that moment in history. They want to see how different and similar they are to those people. They want to imagine themselves in that person's shoes and relate to their experience. This is a great reason to use historical fiction.

- Have a variety of activities. Use lots of different learning opportunities – and not just what you are tempted to default to. Sure, use a textbook, a video, a living book but don't be afraid to think outside the textbook. Make something. Craft something. Draw something. Bake something. Write something. Go somewhere. Talk to someone. Re-enact something. Play a game. Always change it up.

- Make it personal. If there is a way to connect your family to a moment of history, share it with your kids. Were there people in your ancestry who immigrated to Canada? Were any of your family involved in any of the moments of our history? Search your family tree to see how you can dive in more to Canadian history.

It's very important to make sure we consider moments of history from multiple perspectives. Pause in each moment and shift viewpoints in the narrative. How did that moment impact different people and different cultures?

Understanding history is complicated. There are some great questions to ask called the Six Historical Thinking Concepts.

1. Historical Significance: How do we decide what and whose story to tell?

2. Cause & Consequence: What are the causes hidden from view?

3. Continuity & Change: Does change always mean progress?

4. Ethics: What do historical injustices and sacrifices mean to us?

5. Historical Perspectives: How can we ever understand the past?

6. Primary Sources: How do we know what we know?

These are a great place to start conversations alongside your studies of history. You can find out more at the website historicalthinking.ca.

CANADIAN GEOGRAPHY

Canada's geography is amazing. We have such a variety in the landscape from the east coast to the west coast and then up north. We have a mishmash of cultures and peoples. We have huge empty areas of land and large, densely-populated cities. Everything about Canada is diversity.

When people think geography, they usually envision maps and landscape, but it's much more than that. There are two main branches in the study of the earth: physical and human geography. There are also many sub-branches, which includes areas such as cartography, meteorology, urban development, tourism, and more. As homeschoolers, how can we teach all of this to our children in ways that invite curiosity?

Since geography is the study of the world, we need to make sure we include it as part of our learning with our kids. Here are some reasons why:

- It helps us to understand how Canada fits in with the world.

- It gives an appreciation for why some areas are unpopulated while others are very urban — and why cities and towns are built the way they are.

- It creates an opportunity to learn more about your community and region of the country, and to see how it differs from other areas of the country/world.

- It interconnects with teaching Canadian history and understanding how and why people of the past settled where they did and behaved as they did.

- It helps to create awareness of being a good citizen.

SCOPE & SEQUENCE EXAMPLE

Although you can study any subject in any order, sometimes having a general plan of action can be helpful. Here is an example of how to incorporate Canadian content into your learning plans. Remember, this is just a guideline - you can do this however you would like.

Kindergarten / Grade 1

For the very young learner, understanding their local community and how they fit into the bigger picture is a great place to start.

My Community — Discovering more about your community is perfect for these early years.

- What jobs can your children see in the community (police, firefighters, mayor, mechanics, bus drivers, cashiers, librarians, teachers, etc.) and why are they important? What buildings and business are in your community (fire stations, grocery stores, schools, hospitals, restaurants, etc.) and why are they part of the community?

- Walk around your neighbourhood or city centre and draw sketches of what you observe.

- Take the bus or a different-than-usual mode of transportation around your town.

- Chat with different people in the community about their job.

- If you live in an urban area, try to visit somewhere rural. If you live in a rural area, try to visit an urban area. Compare what is the same and what is different in these communities.

Early Mapping Skills — Learning about maps is important. This stage is about learning to read symbols on a map, understanding legends, basic compass understanding of North, East, South, & West, land and water, etc.

- Make a map of your community, either drawing on paper or making 3D models or another creative way.

- Mark the compass points on four walls and play a game where the adult calls out a direction and the kids have to run to that wall.

- Do some basic mapping concept worksheets. There are plenty of these available online to download or in print books like *My Very First Primary Map Book* by Apple Press.

Grades 2 & 3

For later primary grades, it's a good time to have a general introduction of Canada as a country.

An overview of Canada's Geography - Understanding the concepts of provinces and territories.

- Get a good, large map of Canada and put it on the wall or on your table under clear plastic or glass. Reference it often, and look for important places in your life, such as where you live, where other family members live, places you've travelled, etc.

- Exchange postcards from people in other provinces & territories and mark down on the map where they came from.

- Play hands-on and online geography games, and build Canada puzzles.

- Make your own map. Some people like to use salt dough to make a map and add in the physical features. Other people like to draw their maps. You can make a map from LEGO or on Minecraft — whatever is going to work for your studies and personal interests.

- Use technology like Google Earth to explore around the country.

- Keep developing mapping skills — in particular recognizing provinces and their capitals and other important cities, learning to read distances, and expanding on the map skills learned so far.

Canadian Heritage - This is a great place to start understanding about history and timelines, symbols of Canada, and terminology about things related to our country.

- Use a calendar to keep track of birthdays, holidays, and other important events in a visual way to help children understand the idea of timelines.

- Make Canada flag crafts - especially paying attention to the colours and the maple leaf symbol.

- Study Canadian coins and money and talk about what they see on each one. Why is there a beaver, ship, caribou, loon, and polar bear included on our coins? Why is the Queen on the back?

- Join in different cultural events in your community and learn about the diversity of where you live.

- Talk about our Prime Minister, Premiers, and other people in leadership to give kids language to speak about government.

- Read biographies of important Canadians.

General Historical Periods — Do an overview of Canadian history with a focus on various specific moments, such as Indigenous life before the Europeans arrived, life in New France, and pioneers.

- Find out which Indigenous group lives/lived on the lands you currently live on. Study more about their way of life before the Europeans arrived, after, and today.

- If there are any opportunities to speak with an Elder, go and listen.

- Take field trips to museums, historical re-enactment villages, and any other historical centres in your area.

- Try making butter, candles, homemade bread, soap, etc. from scratch like in pioneer days.

- Read historical fiction books that explore these moments of Canadian history more in-depth and have discussions about these experiences.

Grades 4 & 5

In the elementary grades, you can start to explore more about the world and how Canada fits into it, and look at the history of the world.

World Geography - Learn about different cultures and countries of the world.

- Get a great map of the world and put it on the wall or on your table under clear plastic or glass. Reference it often, and look for countries that are important to your family: places you've visited or have family.

- Exchange postcards with people around the world and mark down on the map where they came from.

- Print out the continents of the world and play a game where you have to name the continent and where it is on the world map. Make sure to include positions and names of the oceans as well. Or use a world map puzzle to learn the placement of different countries of the world.

- If there are cultural events near you for different countries, go and visit in person.

- Watch travel guide videos from various countries to get more of an "in-person" view of each place. Listen to the languages spoken and the music created there.

- Read books written about each country.

- Take a virtual trip around the world and "visit" other countries to learn more about them. Find out important features, traditions, peoples, history, landmarks, and other fun things about each country. Make sure to find them on the world map, explore their flag and money, taste-test foods, and whatever else you can find about that country. Use a pretend Canadian passport while you go exploring. You can print out flags or stickers for each country on your visit. Discover how different countries accept visitors from Canada.

World History - Study key events and peoples from around the world.

- Make a timeline of the world and add to it as you progress through history.

- Read quality living books to bring each moment of history to life for your child.

- Tie the historical moments into your world geography lessons by having your child map out the locations of each period you are studying.

- Focus on different cultures and worldviews.

- Watch historical documentaries or movies to make that time period more visual for your child.

- Get as hands-on and creative as possible - make swords and shields, wrap a toga, build LEGO pyramids, see if you can make useful tools out of stone, replicate various styles of art like mosaics and illumination, make dioramas, etc.

Grades 6 – 8

The middle school years are a good time to focus more in-depth on Canada, both our geography and our history - from before the Europeans arrived until the end of the 1800s.

Canadian Geography — Learn more about the province/territory you live in and the rest of the country of Canada, including its physical regions, populations, and cultures.

- Get a quality Canadian atlas that includes detailed information about each province, including their population and industrial details.

- Do a province by province study to learn more about each place. What are they known for? What do they produce, grow, or manufacture? What kinds of people live there? Research landmarks, tourist attractions, and other special things.

- Study the different regions of Canada and what features each has. How do these features affect the people who live there — either as a benefit or a detriment?

- Map out Indigenous Treaties & Tribes. Who do the lands traditionally (and today) belong to?

- Learn when each of the provinces joined Canada.

- Explore geography terms especially relevant to the features we have in Canada.

Canadian History – Take an in-depth look at our history before, during, and after European colonization, usually ending before the beginning of World War I.

- Read living books to bring each moment of history alive, start conversations about various viewpoints, and encourage a more in-depth study.

- Watch historical documentaries such as *Canada, A People's History* or *Canada: The Story of Us* as a jumping point.

- Visit museums, forts, re-enactment centres, or other historical options available near you.

- Make a timeline of history. You can even overlay it from the timeline of world history to see how it all interconnects.

- Be sure to look at moments from all different perspectives and to ask the historical thinking concepts.

- Whenever possible, do something interactive and hands-on - whether that be art, a presentation, an online game, or story-writing.

Grades 9 - 12

In high school, studies about Canada become more detailed and specific.

Some course examples:

- **Canadian Geography**: Focused on the interconnection between natural geography and human geography, creating a more sustainable world, and Canada's part on a global scale.

- **Canada in the 20th Century:** Canada during the first and second World War, the Great Depression, and the aftermath of it all.

- **Civics**: A detailed look at how our government works, and how we relate to each other.

LEARNING ABOUT OUR GOVERNMENT

You can add in studies about how the Canadian government works at any point during your homeschooling journey. However, the best time is during an election period - especially a Federal election. Kids are aware of the promotion that takes place because they can see the candidate signs all over and hear parents talking about various political issues.

Get your kids involved with the election. Talk about different platforms and parties, explain the different stances on various topics, and have your kids decide for themselves who they think would represent them best. Take them voting with you. Let them watch the results and participate in the election process.

The website electionsanddemocracy.ca offers educational tools to help with understanding the voting process. Young learners can participate in a mascot voting activity, while older students can receive an election simulation kit to hold a mock election at home.

YOUR ACTION STEP

Consider if/how you would like to include Canadian resources in your homeschool.

PART IV:

SETTING UP YOUR HOMESCHOOL YEAR

CHAPTER FOURTEEN

PLANNING YOUR HOMESCHOOL YEAR

So you've decided what you are going to be learning this year, how you are going to teach it, then found and bought the curriculum you want to use... now it's time to get it all figured out and organized for the year.

What will your year look like?

When you get ready for a travel adventure, one of the fun parts of preparing is putting together an itinerary — a general plan of where you want to go when. It helps you stay on the path to see and do everything you wanted to along the way. Of course, you can make changes on the fly (and you probably will!). If something exciting comes up or a new opportunity appears along the way, you can decide to adapt the plan -and then get back on track again, if you want to, at a later time.

This is exactly the point of putting together a plan for homeschooling through the year. Planning out your homeschool year is all about breaking it down into smaller chunks so you know what you are doing when, knowing that things can and likely will change.

Having a plan can be helpful when you are tired, down, or feeling behind. It helps when you are dealing with multiple kids, someone gets sick, or you have to take time off and wonder where you were when you come back.

Before the plan can be put into place, some thought is needed on how you want to lay out your year. There are so many different ways you can run your week and your year. You need to pick what will work for you and your family.

- Do you want to follow the traditional school year — September through June, with the same holidays and breaks?

- Do you want to school for only 4 days a week, keeping one day off for field trips, playdates, errands, etc.?

- Do you want to school on the weekends or not?

- Do you want to do "Sabbath School" which is 6 weeks of school followed by a resting 7th week off?

- Do you want to spread your school work out throughout the year and do year-round schooling with time off as you'd like through the year?

- Are there times and days in your year that you will need to have off?

Get these ideas together first. Having the timeframe to work around makes putting the plan into place much easier.

A common method new homeschoolers try to do is to follow the structure of a public school system. Believing that they need to complete several subjects a day within specific time frames, they try to put together a firm plan. The problem is that often this level of structure isn't able to be replicated at home. It tends to lead to stress and frustration, especially if your days don't go according to the plan.

This is part of the reason behind deschooling - to realize that home education can and should be different than the school system. We have the freedom to find a way that works for us instead of trying to force ourselves to do things a specific way.

BLOCKING AND LOOPING

There are two basic methods for planning out your homeschool year.

The first is called block planning - where you plan to put specific subjects on specific days. It's when you know that every Tuesday and Thursday you are doing history and every Wednesday and Friday you are doing science, for example. Each day has a planned block of learning.

The second is called looping. This is where you have a plan for each subject but instead of scheduling things on a specific day, you just do the next thing on the list. Using the time you've set aside for school, you work your way down the list, stopping whenever your school time ends. The next day, you pick up the list and continue where you left off. When you get to the bottom of the list, you head back to the top and start again. You work in a looping pattern.

Of course, you can always merge these two plans to come up with a hybrid plan that is perfectly adapted to your family's needs.

The important thing to remember is that there is no right or wrong way to schedule your homeschool day, there's only the right way to do it for you.

IF YOU CHOOSE TO BLOCK PLAN

Choosing a Planner

There are lots of different ways and methods for planners — options for DIY, digital, printed, and pre-made. You can just use a spreadsheet. You can make a bullet journal with your plans. You can use online homeschool or lesson planners such as Homeschool Planet, Homeschool Panda, or PlanBook. You can buy a pre-printed teacher's lesson planner. You can download a planner from a homeschool blogger or Etsy. I can't tell you which one to use because this is a pretty personal preference. Look at all your options and see which one feels like the best fit for you.

Some people like planners to have specific dates on them, whereas others feel very trapped and panicky because if they miss a day their lessons are all messed up. If you are the latter, I recommend changing the date to Day 1, Day 2, Day 3 instead of specific calendar dates. Then if you miss a day, you still are on schedule because it's by day number instead!

Another tip if you are using a printed planner and are writing things in: use a pencil. That way it's editable and you can move things around as needed. Make sure any digital planner you have also offers a drag and drop option so you can change it as you want.

Making the Itinerary

When you have chosen a planner and know how you need or want the year laid out, it's time to plunk the information in.

Some curricula have suggested schedules included, so take that plan (if it works for you) and simply drop it into the planner. If it doesn't work for you, or there isn't a schedule, go through the program and break it down into chunks.

Traditional school years are typically broken up into 36 weeks or 180 days. Of course, this is just a guideline, but it can be helpful when you need to figure out how to schedule your plans. Break things down and add them to the planner. Do one thing at a time until you have everything down and — tada! Lessons all planned!

Remember, a planner is not a ball and chain. It's just a visual way to see what you are working on and a guideline to help you reach the goals you set out for the year. Homeschooling is about flexibility. If you end up doing an unplanned road trip to the grandparents for a week mid-year and get knocked off your plan — there's no need to be worried. The plan isn't set in stone. It's supposed to be a helpful tool. If any part of it is stressing you out or weighing you down, drop it.

IF YOU CHOOSE TO LOOP PLAN:

Loop scheduling takes the pressure off needing to do a specific thing at a specific time. With block scheduling, if you miss a science lesson on day 2, you might need to shuffle things around to fit it in somewhere else or skip it until next week or cram extra lessons into one day to stay on task. With loop scheduling, you just pick up where you left off.

At its simplest form, loop scheduling is just writing down a list of all the subjects you want to complete and then working your way down the list, returning to the top when you get to the end. If you skip a day of "school," you just pick up where you left off and keep chipping away at the list.

For example, your loop may look something like this:

- math

- language

- science

- history

- art

- French

- spelling

Let's say you've set aside 2 hours of learning every day. On Monday, you start with math since it's first on the list. You take as long as you need to finish the lesson for math. If there is time remaining in your school period, you move to language and start that lesson until you are done school for the day. On Tuesday, you pick up where you left off. If that means finishing up the language lesson, you start there, then move to science and then history. This continues through the week until you've finished spelling. Then it's back to math. Over and over again.

If you have subjects you need or want to spend more time on, simply add them more frequently to the looping list so you focus on them more often.

Instead of using a planner, you might find it easier with this looping method to make lesson lists. Break down the subject lessons the same as in the block schedule, but don't put it into a calendar format. Write every lesson for each subject into its own list and cross it off as it is completed through your loop.

COMBINING LOOP AND BLOCK PLANNING

It is possible to combine both planning styles to create a schedule that is both scheduled and flexible. There may be some subjects, such as math, reading, and spelling, that you want to do every day. These would be your blocked subjects. You put them in the plan and they stay there. Then you can loop all the other subjects you would like. This allows you to still have flexibility within your day while making sure you focus on the subjects you feel need daily touchpoints.

IF YOU HATE PLANNING OR YOU'VE DECIDED TO UNSCHOOL

If you feel completely trapped by the thought and use of a planner — don't feel overwhelmed or discouraged. There are some other options.

- You can write down a plan every day or every week instead of the whole year if that's too much.

- Record retroactively. Instead of planning, you can document what you've done. This is especially useful for unschooling families who don't have a set plan but still want to keep track of learning. At the end of the day (or throughout the day, if that's easier), simply write down in a notebook what you did that day. What activities did you do? What learning took place? What resources did you use? Add in notes or comments - especially from your child.

To be honest, one of the best tips I've heard is that you just need to "Do The Next Thing." Turn the next page in your book. Start the next lesson. Move onto the next level. Just keep going.

PULLING IT ALL TOGETHER

At this point, it's about making the actual implementation of the plan easier. Since you know what you are going to teach and when, you can spend some time putting systems in place, so you are all set and ready to go for the year.

- Print and sort everything. Print out any worksheets or photocopy the pages you will need and put them in file folders for the week or day they are supposed to be in. If the thought or cost of printing out a year's worth of paperwork ahead of time is too much, try doing a month or a week at a time. The idea is to not have to remember the day of, so you aren't running around getting things ready at the last minute.

- Make a book list per week so you know what to get at the library before you need it.

- Buy your supplies. Get some good pencils, art materials, and any other school supplies you need. Get any science experiment materials you require and put them in a container. Get your workbooks or binders and anything else you are going to need this year.

- Set up accounts on any websites you need and put the passwords somewhere to reference as needed.

GETTING ORGANIZED

If you've ever lived out of a backpack, you know the importance of learning how to carefully pack your bag. Everything has a specific place it needs to be stored. Things need to be folded in a specific way so you can maximize the space you have.

Homeschooling is the same way. The best plan is to know where things need to go to keep it organized. Let's talk about some ways to help avoid homeschool chaos taking over your home.

Many new homeschoolers are tempted to create a space in their home that will be designated as the "homeschool room." They envision desks, shelves, and other traditional school-style decor. Although there is nothing wrong with this plan, you will likely find that over time, you just use your kitchen or dining room table. (Or the couch. Or the floor. Or the bed. Or the patio. Or the trampoline. Or…)

Avoid the temptation of spending large amounts of money on furniture and supplies off the start. Wait until you settle into your homeschooling styles and routine to see what would work best for your family.

My one recommendation is to find a shelf or space for everyone (including you as the teacher) to consistently keep your books and supplies. Knowing where to find things to get started and where things go when school is done is super helpful to make your day run smoothly.

Set up a system for your resources. Have a way to make it easy for you and your kids to grab what is needed. If you have multiple children, give each kid a box or bin with their "stuff" in it. Consider colour coding and/ or decorative patterned tape to label things per kid to make it even easier.

We have found the best way to keep all our stuff organized is with some collapsible bins from the dollar store. Each child gets their own. Inside they have any workbooks for the year, a binder to store any loose-leaf papers they use, and any child-specific resource they will need. A pencil case keeps their favourite pencil, eraser, glue stick, and scissors nearby. I try to match the colour of their notebooks with their accessories so I can remember who left their scissors on the table at the end of the day.

In the middle of the island, I have a cup or a mason jar full of extra pencils, an extra eraser, and a pencil sharpener. That way, whenever a child inevitably loses their pencil, there is quick access to another one.

The idea is to make everything easy to find, easy to use, and easy to clean up - however that works for your family.

AND FINALLY - BREATHE

Remember — the most important thing for a homeschool year is to enjoy learning. All the homeschool planning the world is pointless if you are always fighting or struggling or hating every minute. Just use these planning steps to help you succeed in your year, not to feel trapped by a plan. Enjoy learning with your kids, however that works for you.

YOUR ACTION STEP

Decide if you want to use a block or loop plan - or a combination of both - for your homeschool year and put together the plan. OR, if you have decided to unschool, find a great notebook or calendar to keep track of what you've completed each day.

CHAPTER FIFTEEN
HOW TO SCHEDULE YOUR HOMESCHOOL DAY

As with all things homeschooling, flexibility is one of the greatest benefits. Ask a group of homeschoolers how they run their days and you will get a different answer for each of them.

A common approach is to do structured learning in the morning followed by free time in the afternoon. This allows for things like quiet time, playdates, field trips, classes and co-ops, personal interest activities, and a plethora of other things.

Intentional learning time when you homeschool is much shorter than at public school. You usually do not need to plan a 9 am to 3 pm school day when you choose to learn at home.

A schedule is defined as "*a series of things to be done or events to occur at or during a particular time or period.*"

In school terms, a morning tends to look something like:

- 9:00 to 9:30 — spelling
- 9:30 to 10:00 — math
- 10:00 to 10:15 - snack
- 10:15 to 10:45 - French
- 10:45 to 11:15 - science
- 11:15 to 12:00 - independent reading

While this has a place in our lives, running our homeschool by such a structure can often put stress on our days and push us into a sense of failure. What if math takes longer than 30 minutes today? What if we end up struggling with spelling and everything falls behind? It can make your kids feel like they aren't meeting expectations.

I've found when we've tried to do things with these time structures, I am more frustrated and snappy with my kids, and they push back harder since they feel trapped.

I am a big advocate for routine over schedule. Routines take the idea of a plan and give it more flex room. It uses an approach I like to call the "And Then..." approach, like this:

Wake up, and then have breakfast, and then do math, and then do spelling, and then have a snack, and then read, and then do some chores.

We know what comes next without having the clock dictate each moment of the day. It provides freedom with guidelines.

At our house, we intentionally set aside our weekday mornings for learning. We use a simple block schedule for our plans so the kids are familiar with what to expect each day, such as knowing they have to do a lesson of math every morning.

DAILY PLANS

Having a way for your kids to visually see what they are expected to accomplish in their day is a great way to get them on board, avoid arguments, and make it easy for them to develop independence. Here are a few ways to do that:

A Checklist

A terrific and simple way to have a daily plan is to write down what you want done in the day and let your child check things off as finished. Don't forget you can add chores and out-of-the-house activities too!

Some great ideas for this are to use:

- a student planner where they have the school plan written in to keep track of what to do each day

- a whiteboard to write the list and erase when done

- a paper checklist — either in a notebook or on a single piece of paper

- a digital list with checkboxes in a program like Excel or an app like Trello

Visual Charts

Sometimes, seeing pictures is the best way to understand what needs to be done in the day. Make cards with each subject on them and have your child flip them over as they complete their work. It's an easy way for a child to see their progress.

Workbox System

Several years ago, there was a buzz in the homeschool community about a method of daily organization called "workboxes." Created by a woman named Sue Patrick, the basic plan is that you have a set of containers of some sort, and label each with a number using Velcro dots.

Each bin is filled with subject by subject work to do, or a snack or free play, or chore cards, or whatever you need. Your child starts at bin 1 and when finished what is inside, moves that Velcro number to a chart and then starts on bin 2. They repeat until all the bins are done for the day.

You need to reset the bins every day, but it's a way to teach your child some independence.

MORNING BASKETS

Morning baskets are a popular way to add family learning time to your homeschooling day. But what is a morning basket and how do you use it?

The concept of the morning basket is derived from the ideals of the Charlotte Mason homeschooling method, but it is easily adaptable to many different styles of education. It might also be called circle time or morning meeting. The basic idea is to bring everyone together and do some learning as a family or group.

A morning basket is an easy way to include topics you might otherwise forget or skip in your learning, review what you've been learning so far, connect and chat with each other, memorize things, read books, and touch on subjects that are of importance to your family. All the resources needed to work through this time are kept in a basket or something portable so it is easy to transport as needed and easy to access. The goal is to have a relaxed, fun, simple time together covering different things for short periods.

Just like homeschooling is unique for every family, a morning basket is going to look different for everyone. What one family will include might not be in another family's morning basket. Some people feel that everything you do with your kids in morning basket time should be quality literature and book-based studies. Other people are more relaxed and use a variety of resources to make their morning times personalized. You need to decide what works for your learning goals and your family.

Here are a few common examples of things you might want to include:

- a read-aloud book

- poetry

- art appreciation

- music appreciation

- character study

- Bible reading (for faith-based homeschoolers)

- memorization (of poems or book passages or Bible verses)

- prayers or meditation time

- audio stories

- review of lessons learned

Some other ideas include:

- history or geography

- health

- French or another second language

- the National Anthem

- fitness breaks (like yoga or activity challenge cards)

- mindfulness activities

- team-building exercises

- math flashcards

- brain teasers / puzzles

- conversation starters

You can plan out activities in your morning basket the same way you plan your year - either with a block schedule or on a looping plan. Just remember to keep everything short. Activities should only be 10-15 minutes each and vary between activities. For example, a period of listening to a story might be followed by a hands-on art activity, which could be followed by an open discussion about a picture of a famous painting, and then another read aloud.

How people use a morning basket is as individualized as the content included in it. Some people decide to use a morning basket right at the start of the day, completing all the things inside said basket before moving on to individual studies and activities. Other people spread it throughout the day, breaking it up into chunks of learning at different times. Some people use the read-alouds and other activities that involve sitting around at mealtimes when their audience is captivated and available to sit still for a few minutes. The morning basket can be used as the primary core of your homeschool day or it can be a small extra — it's dependent on your family and how you run your school.

Morning baskets are not mandatory. They are just one option some families enjoy.

Although our family has never been as intentional or consistent with morning time as I may have liked over the years, for a while we did use a routine of gathering together in the morning to have what we called Morning Meeting. The goal was to have everyone up, fed, and ready to go by 9 am when I called them to the living room couch. This was a time of day where we all gathered together and talked about concerns or ideas — kind of like a family meeting. We discussed things coming up that day or week. It was my chance to connect with my gang as a family and allow us to intentionally spend time together. As the years have passed, we have somewhat fallen away from this habit and chat together at meal times instead.

Homeschooling is all about individualization. Pick the ideas that sound like they may work for you and drop the ones that won't.

YOUR ACTION STEP

Figure out a routine for your days that fits your family, your lifestyle, and the curriculum that you've chosen.

CHAPTER SIXTEEN

HOMESCHOOLING MULTIPLE CHILDREN

Many homeschooling families have more than one child and wonder how exactly to tackle the challenge of education with them all.

WHEN YOU TEACH MULTIPLE GRADES

If you have children in a variety of grades, you can approach learning from two perspectives: finding a way to study together in a group or rotating learning.

Group Learning

If your children can sit and learn together, group study is a wonderful way to homeschool. Even in a group with wide age gaps, you can learn the main lesson together and then each child can complete an assignment or task related to that main lesson.

The idea is to take the bulk of the heavy teaching and do it once, then branch out with more age-appropriate activities with each child.

For example, you can read a book and watch a video with all of your children about a topic. Then, your preschooler can colour a picture while your elementary student writes a short paragraph about the topic and your high schooler does more research to put together an essay.

It works well for any "extra" topics you want to cover, such as the arts, a second language, and religious studies, but can also be used for the main form of learning subjects like science and social studies. Math - probably not.

Some advantages of group learning are:

- simplifying your day because you only need to teach once for all

- spending more time learning together as a family

- having conversations about the topics you are learning about outside of school time, with everyone able to participate.

Some disadvantages are:

- difficulty using this method if you have kids of varying learning needs or behavioral issues

- times older kids feel their learning isn't challenging enough because it's designed for multiple ages

- chaos among kids who tend to fight.

Rotate Children

The other option is to set up a plan so you connect with each child in turn to do intentional learning times.

As an example, if you have four children (a preschooler, a Grade 1, a Grade 6, and a Grade 8 - let's say), your school time might look something like this:

1. Spend some time with the preschooler before you start school with the other kids, doing intentional reading or workbooks or activities together. Then they can go play or sit beside you to work on a puzzle or colouring book.

2. Do schoolwork with the Grade 1 child at the kitchen table as the Grade 6 and Grade 8 students work independently.

3. When Grade 1 is done for the day, you sit down with Grade 6. You check the work they've been doing to make sure they are doing it right and understand. You complete any subjects that need one on one work - like spelling or science or read alouds, etc.

4. When that child is done, you repeat the same tasks with the Grade 8 student. After lunch, you snuggle on the couch with your preschooler and read or do a special learning time together again.

The idea of this plan is to touch base with each child one at a time, confirm what they've been working on to make sure they are on task, and then do anything specific that needs a teacher to guide them through learning.

Some advantages of rotational learning:

- It intentionally connects you with each child and confirms they understand what they have been learning.

- It gives you more flexibility in personalizing a learning plan for each child.

Some disadvantages:

- It requires your children to be able to find things to do while you work with another child one on one.

- It may take more time, especially if you have lots of children.

- You tend to sit in one place for a longer time since you are the centre of the action.

Either option can work to help you teach multiple children. You can even combine both ideas by starting your day together with any extra subjects and then do one-on-one for core subjects.

Having a plan and preparation in place makes the experience of having a wide range of children in your homeschool much less of a stress and more of a joy.

WHEN YOU HAVE LITTLE CHILDREN, TOO

Trying to homeschool with little ones around can be a challenge. Preschoolers, toddlers, and babies simply require a lot more time, attention, and support than older children do and are quite the demand on your focus. It can be hard to figure out how, exactly, to successfully meet their needs while still teaching their siblings. Let's talk about how you can do homeschooling when you have little kids too.

Teach older children independence in learning.

Although older children will still need help in their homeschool education, giving them the ability to be more independent means you aren't tied to their side for however long it takes them to finish the work they are supposed to be doing in a day. Give your older kids freedom to succeed at independence by offering the daily checklists of what they need to accomplish. Let them work alone on subjects they can do without your guided help when you need to focus on their younger siblings. Use online resources that they can complete without you. This doesn't mean you aren't available or able to help, but you can meet the needs of more kids at once.

Ask older children to help.

If you have multiple older children, ask an older child to be "in charge" of their younger siblings for a short time while you do some one-on-one work with another child. That caregiver-child can do anything from reading to the little one to LEGO creating to just simply playing. As long as they know they are to make sure their little sibling is safe, and not getting into trouble, it can be a big relief.

Use technology.

As our world becomes more and more digital, so many amazing resources for all ages are becoming available. There are some incredible resources for our youngest children that are fun, interactive, and educational. Pull out a tablet and let them use an app for a short time. Turn on the computer and let them play or watch clips of their favourite television shows. Give them a toy computer that has some games on it.

Never underestimate the power of a TV show, either. If your little one will focus for the 20 minutes of a kid show, it means you know where they are and what they are doing for a small chunk of time that you can use to work one-on-one with an older child. This can be a lifesaver when that little one is being particularly challenging or needy while you are trying to get through school.

Fill up their tanks first.

Before you start the school day with your older kids (or when they are working independently), spend some quality time with your smallest family members. Sit on the couch with a book and snuggle. Make muffins together. Do something to help them feel happy and content and special, instead of needing to vie for your attention. Intentionally filling their little love tanks before moving onto the next child can make a huge improvement in their ability to keep busy without you while you work with other kids.

Give them something special to do.

Having special activities they are only allowed to do while it's school time usually excites the little ones. Here are some ideas:

Whiteboard. For me, this is a great, no-brainer kind of activity because little ones stay close by, practice fine motor skills, learn to draw shapes and letters, and discover what happens when they mix colours. It allows for creativity. As long as the markers stay off the carpet and clothes, this is a quick and mess-free activity.

Busy bags. That's exactly what they are. Zippered bag with activities inside to keep your little one busy while working on a skill. Usually, each bag focuses on something specific like fine motor skills, colour recognition, numbers or letters, etc. The child opens the bag, does the activity, puts it back in the bag, and then moves onto the next one. There are zillions of ideas for busy bags on sites like Pinterest.

Reading cozy corner. Set up a little kid reading space with kid-sized chairs, or a pile of pillows and blankets, etc. and add a small bin of books. Give them opportunities to go sit in their special space and read. Rotating those books frequently means it will hold your child's attention more often.

Special toy bin. Find a toy or set of toys that are only available for times when you are doing school with your older kids. Again, these can be rotated to keep their attention and interest.

Housework. Now, I'm not suggesting that your toddler or preschooler is likely going to be able to do much that will make a big dent in your housekeeping list, but they do love feeling special and helpful by doing housekeeping tasks. Pass them a duster or a small broom. Give them a cloth and a spray bottle of water to wash the windows or cupboard doors. Get them to match socks or shoes. Have them unload the cutlery from the dishwasher into the right spaces in the drawer. (I put my cutlery drawer on the floor so they can see inside without having to climb something.)

Art. Crayons and paper can be a toddler's heaven. Print out colouring pages with their favourite animals and characters, and keep them close at hand for a short attention grabber for your little ones. Put some poster paint into a zippered bag, tape it to the table, and allow them to finger paint without the mess. Get some of those Crayola Magic Markers that only colour on special paper (no mess!) Make playdough for them. Give them stickers.

Trays. Set up a special station where you can put together trays just for your little one. They can either be educational trays (often called Tot Trays) or you can try a Montessori tray that focuses more on learning a practical skill like pouring water into a cup or cutting paper.

Tinker box. Fill up a box with miscellany (straws, popsicles sticks, tape, paper scraps, etc.) and let them be self-led engineers.

Sensory bin. Pour some coloured rice or noodles in a bin or a cake pan. Make cloud dough or playdough. Cut up streamers. Add ice to some water. Use whatever hands-on thing they can put their hands into! Add some utensils and let them play.

Let them do "school."

Although they don't need to do any sense of formal learning until they are older, young ones always seem to be the most eager to participate in school. Buying cheap workbooks for them to scribble in (or attempt to work on without pressure) can give them the sense of being part of the school fun their older siblings are doing. Educational activities they can do at the table can be a fun way to learn. Print off extra copies of things you print for your older children so they can scribble away at it too. Do a modified preschool program for them so they have "real" work to do at the same time.

Break up school into chunks.

If you are finding you need more time for your little ones because they keep interrupting school time, break the day up into smaller chunks. Instead of tackling everything on the list in one big go, do one thing at a time with your school-aged kids then take a short break to focus on the younger ones. Repeat.

Put them somewhere safe.

One of the biggest frustrations with toddlers and preschoolers is their uncanny ability to get into anything in no time flat. You just turn your head for a minute and there is a huge mess.

Finding a safe environment while you need to focus on something else is important. For the really little ones, that might mean a playpen. Do your schoolwork in a single room of the house and add baby gates or close the door or just have your younger child beside you at the table or on the couch to keep them close.

ACTION STEP

If you have multiple children, figure out whether group learning or rotations will work best for your family. If you have little ones, decide which of these tips you can impliment to make your day run smoothly.

PART V:
THE MYTH OF BALANCE

CHAPTER SEVENTEEN
LEARNING TO PRIORITIZE

Homeschooling involves a lot of parts: research, planning, prepping, buying/selling, teaching, evaluating, etc. All of these parts together can take up a lot of your time. If you have multiple kids, multiply the time and energy needed by that number. It's easy to get caught in this perpetual hamster wheel of never-ending thinking about homeschooling.

But if homeschooling becomes your main or only focus, as with anything on our priority list, other things get missed. We will become blind to the fact that we've forgotten to enjoy fun time together as a family. We will ignore our own self-care needs.

We too often let our homeschooling experience be led by fear. Fear we are failing our children. Fear of judgement. Fear of comparison. It feeds off our insecurities. This can quickly lead us to an obsession to succeed, perform, and strive for goals that are unrealistic for our kids.

We cannot let our role as teacher supersede our role as parent, spouse, or friend. It's just one of our hats, not our only hat.

THE MYTH OF BALANCE

Balance. The word itself conjures up images of wait staff holding trays of heavy, precariously perched glasses and dishes, swiftly weaving between the tables as they deliver their orders. Or maybe that of a gymnast nimbly jumping and dancing across a narrow beam with grace and elegance. Perhaps you envision the gentle, carefully measured procedure of stacking objects onto a scale in an attempt to achieve a perfectly equal level.

When you look up the word balance in the dictionary, some of the definitions include:

- *stability produced by even distribution of weight on each side of the vertical axis*

- *equipoise between contrasting, opposing, or interacting elements*

- *physical equilibrium*

- *mental and emotional steadiness*

There is a popular belief that, if you do things properly, it is possible to find a way to balance all the sections and responsibilities in our lives so they each get the time they need and we find success/peace/happiness. We are expected to be able to do everything to the fullest.

Here's the truth: Balance is a myth.

Life is more about priorities, flexibility, and simplification than balance. In a world where we are pulled in a thousand different directions, it is impossible to accomplish this mysterious idea of equilibrium — let alone the idea that we can be mentally and emotionally steadfast. Trying to do EVERYTHING is just a way to lead to stress, burnout, and failure.

As homeschoolers, we choose to put the education of our children as a priority. But we also have a lot of other things we are responsible for:

feeding the family, maintaining our homes, taking care of our well-being, work, etc.

Can we do it all and if so, how? Do we need to?

Prioritizing things in our life makes us conscious of what we should be focusing on instead of letting ourselves just wing it and hope for the best. As homeschoolers with many pulls in different directions, it's essential to figure out what is important to us and what isn't.

There is a meme that appears on social media frequently among my mommy friends. It's a triangle with the words "Pick Two." At each corner of the triangle is an option: family, clean house, sanity. I think it is a fairly apt representation of life, although I probably wouldn't use a triangle. I'd probably end up with a weirdly uneven multi-pointed shape instead, with family, work, and homeschool near the top and housework and self-care at the bottom.

We have so many things that demand our time and attention. Choosing the things that are most important to us is vital. That way we don't end up trying to do everything and fail at most things. Being intentional with our time is the best way to be successful. So, let's figure out which things are the most important for us to prioritize.

Step 1. Make a list.

Write down all the things that vie for your time. Think of everything: housework, family time, your work, where you volunteer, homeschooling, all the places you have to get kids to, groups you belong to, self-care time, etc.

Step 2. Get Rid of Extras.

Think if there is anything you can take off that list. If you are feeling overwhelmed with all the responsibilities in your life, you will likely need to remove some things. Seriously consider everything you've written down. Is there anything you can see right away that you can (or should) cross off? Get rid of the extras that are dragging you down. It's okay to say no and to give up things that are weighing you down. If you don't want to do it and don't have to do it, then don't. Cross off everything you are taking off the list. Give yourself freedom.

Step 3. Prioritize.

Now that you've pared down your list to things that you have to or need to keep on it, it's time to decide what order of importance each needs to have. You need to decide what things are important for you and your family.

Priorities for me might not be the same for you. For example, in my house, I'd say my priorities are kids, husband, homeschool, and my work. Housekeeping, on the other hand, is wayyyyy down on my list of importance.

A short note here is to remember this isn't a "set in stone," forever and ever kind of prioritization list. You can change plans for the day based on the current priorities. This is just intended to help make the flow and rhythm of your life easier.

Make your way down the list and number things in priority order, or make stars beside the ones that are vital to you.

Step 4. Block time.

We have talked a little about blocking intentional chunks of time for things to make sure you put the important things into your day.

Before considering any extras, go through the list you just prioritized and put the things you know you need or want to do on your plan for each day/week/month.

For example, homeschooling being a priority, you might purposefully set each weekday morning aside to complete formal learning. You might decide to set aside an hour every Friday afternoon for the bulk of your housekeeping. If you have a planner for your days, you can use different coloured pens or pencil crayons to block out time in a visual way.

Then follow the plan.

This can be the hardest part, especially if you are like me and are easily sidetracked or get too focused on things.

Step 5. Use hacks, tips, shortcuts, and systems for the extras.

For the things you don't want to spend extended time on, or can't commit yourself to, find a way to accomplish them "well-enough" through the use of hacks, tips, shortcuts, and systems. We'll dive into some suggestions for these in the next few chapters.

Step 6. Evaluate.

Use your system and see how it works.

- Do you find you are better able to handle everything you need to do?

- Is there anything that's not working?

- Have you noticed anything that was missed on your schedule or that you've allotted too much time to?

- What changes can you make?

If you are finding it hard to keep on task or have something that keeps you from focusing on the most important things on your priority list, you might want to find an accountability partner. Having to tell someone what you've done all day can make you aware of how you use your time.

Now, let's talk about how to hack these systems.

YOUR ACTION STEP

Complete this prioritization step. Figure out what is important to include in your days and cut out all the extras.

CHAPTER EIGHTEEN

HOUSEWORK AND HOMESCHOOLING

My favourite quote about housekeeping is, "Cleaning your house while you have kids is like trying to brush your teeth while eating Oreos." Since we homeschool, we are home more and make more messes to clean up. It often feels like a lost cause.

Housekeeping (laundry, cleaning, meal planning, etc.) is so far down on my priority list that it is almost not on the list. Unfortunately, cutting it out completely would be unacceptable and have negative health consequences, so I'm kind of obligated to do it. But I hate it. All of it.

To make sure I'm successful at doing housekeeping, I use a few tricks. Here are five ways to be more victorious at homeschooling and housekeeping.

Whenever you can, have a plan. That means meal plans, cleaning plans, homeschool plans, shopping plans... everything and anything. A plan can make potentially stressful and hard situations much simpler.

Meals

Some people love to know everything they are going to eat for each meal for an entire year. Some people like to look in the fridge/freezer and plan that morning. Others look in the cupboard at 5 pm and wonder what to make before the kids throw a mutiny.

Having a meal plan together is amazing, freeing, and (sometimes) more cost-efficient. Looking at the list and seeing what you have to make for supper that night means you don't have to think. It's just one less stress off your plate. All you need to do in the morning is make sure you have the pre-prep stuff done — like take the meat out to thaw or throw things in a slow cooker. Knowing what you are going to eat for the week can help you save money when you go grocery shopping because you are less likely to buy extras, plus you don't need to get takeout unless you planned to.

There are LOTS of places to find meal plans. Pinterest is a terrific tool to find plans made and shared by other people or recipes you might want to include. Apps like PrePear, PlateJoy, or Paprika offer meal plans at your fingertips.

Of course, you can also just make one up yourself. Make a list of all the meals you know your family likes, pop them into a calendar and ta-da! Meal plan. If you want to take it a step further, put all the ingredients for each meal on a list for the week – either on paper you can print out or an app you can take with you on your phone. This makes grocery shopping easier too.

Housekeeping

There are plenty of options available to help you keep a schedule on your housekeeping. If you are good with making your own system, go for it.

If you need help, as I do, there are some well-established programs people use with success.

- **FlyLady.net** — This system is a very popular one and lots of people have found great success using the FlyLady method. There are daily tasks, journaling, routines to establish, monthly habits to work on, and a community of people to be encouraged with. At the very least, you will have a shiny sink.

- **MotivatedMoms.com** — This cleaning program includes either an app or access to a collection of printable options of daily task checklists. All you have to do is look at the list, do what it says each day, and check things off when complete. It's simple and easy to keep on top of.

Use Available Services.

As life in our society gets busier and people have less time to do the things they need to, more and more services are popping up to help. Why not use them to your advantage?

- **Grocery Services**

Look for a local grocery store where you can order online and either go pick up or have your groceries delivered. You are able to skip the time in the store, plus you can save serious money too because you won't be tempted to grab spontaneous extras!

- **Cleaning Services**

If you hate cleaning and can afford to, pay someone else to clean your house for you. It can take a big weight off your shoulders.

- **Errand Runners**

There are great people out there who have made their businesses around running errands for other people. This can be a great solution to that long list of things that just seem to suck up all your time in a day.

INCLUDING THE KIDS

If the kids are part of the family, it's a good chance they are part of the reason for the housekeeping, right? Toys, clutter, clothes, dishes, books, stuff — it all just seems to pile up. I know sometimes it's a challenge to convince them to help and feel like their efforts are actually helpful, but getting the kids involved is a great way to keep on top of tasks. Plus, it helps them develop skills for their future.

Chores

There are lots of ideas to help you implement and encourage your kids to do their share around the house.

One method that worked successfully in our home was to make cards for each room of the house with a checklist of the things I expected done in that room. The kids pick a card, do the tasks, then flip the card upside down when done.

Another method has been to write out the list of jobs for the day on a whiteboard and let the kids decide which they will each be willing and able to do for the day, then be accountable to finish them properly.

You will need to find a method that works for you and your kids.

Teach Them to Do It Alone

Ideally, getting the kids to do things for you would be perfect. Teach them the skills they need to do the tasks that take up too much of your time. Add home economics to your lessons. Teach them cooking skills so they can make supper. Teach them how to do laundry, buy groceries, complete small house repairs, and do all the extras around the house so you can hand over the reins.

Organize

One trick I find helpful is to find homes for everything. If everyone knows where something belongs, it's less likely to end up in a pile somewhere or all over the table or floor. Things need designated places. Admittedly, this is an eternal work in progress in my home, and then just when I think I have everything figured out, something pops up that mixes this up again. BUT when things are settled, it is much easier and faster to clean things up.

Purging things that fill your home with clutter and chaos can help you feel more at peace.

The secret to good housekeeping is just to do it and keep at it. Every single step you take makes progress.

YOUR ACTION STEP

Consider which of these time savers you can add to your days.

CHAPTER NINETEEN

WORKING AND HOMESCHOOLING

Working and homeschooling can be a challenging scenario for a homeschooling family when the parents have to work. Is it possible to successfully homeschool this way? Absolutely! But again, this requires evaluation of priorities and intentional time planning.

Whether you work outside the home or at home, juggling the needs of a job with the desires of homeschooling can be a tough one. Both require extreme demands on your time, attention, and commitment. You need to do some good planning to make it happen.

WORKING OUTSIDE THE HOME

If you work outside the home, the first major thing you need to consider is childcare. If your child is too young to stay home alone and your spouse, if you have one, isn't home either, you will need someone to watch them.

Some ideas:

- another family member, such as a grandparent

- a friend

- another homeschool family

- a nanny or au-pair

- child care centre

Once you have that in place, the next thing to figure out is the learning plan.

Although you are more than able to use any homeschool method or curriculum you like, if you are working out of the home you have a few extra questions to consider.

For example, you will want to look at how much parent involvement there is for each option. Look at how much prep work, planning, and teaching will need to be done by you and consider if that's going to be realistic given your working schedule.

You may want to look at resources that allow your children to work more independently, such as online programs.

It's important to remember that learning happens all the time and that, as homeschoolers, you have flexibility in what "school" looks and feels like. There is no requirement as to what time of day or which day of the week school needs to happen. Fit it in however works for you.

For example, if you have someone in your home to care for your child throughout the day and they are willing to take on some of the teaching role for you — that is one option. You can also do more formal schoolwork whenever you are off. Evenings, holidays, and weekends are perfectly valid options for school time.

If your child is old enough and responsible enough to stay home alone, you can leave them a list of work for the day. Make sure they know what they need to do and check in with them regularly. For example, use programs like Google Hangouts or Facebook Messenger for kids to touch base throughout the day on your breaks. Have a plan for what to do if they get stuck on something during the day. They should also have a place to put their completed work for a daily check-in with you later. Regular meetings are vital to make sure your child is on track and understands what they are learning.

Another important thing to consider is internet safety. If you aren't home all day, make sure your kids are safe online. Find a good internet filter option.

Working and homeschooling are both possible but will take some maneuvering and fan-dangling to find the perfect solution for your family.

WORKING AT HOME

Working at home has a different set of needs. Without that physical break of being in a different location for work, it's easy to get pulled in many directions and find yourself interrupted frequently by the needs of your family.

Find a time where you can focus on work. Working amid a homeschool life might not allow you to close the office door and sit to do focused work for hours, but intentionally blocking a chunk of time for your primary focus to be on work is key.

For me, I get up early and attempt to work until 8:30 or so and then again in the mid-afternoon until supper time. I use that time to chip away on my work to-do lists, but I'm still a mom. I still have parenting requirements (getting meals, handling sibling squabbles, changing the TV channel 1000 times until I can find the particular show they want, etc.)

But between all the parenting, I know what I'm working on. I have a list of work stuff at my desk so I can sit down and focus. It's easier to have a designated time frame intentionally set for working. Even interrupted, I can still cross off lots of things on that list.

One big temptation is to do work while the kids do school. I highly recommend making a rule for yourself that school time is not work time. Dividing your attention means your kids aren't getting the best of you and neither is your work. Put the phone out of reach, close the laptop, block social media, etc. Focus on the kids and give them the best learning time.

If you can afford it, find an assistant who can do some of the time-consuming but non-essential tasks on your worklist. What tasks you can outsource will depend on the kind of business you have. Commonly outsourced tasks include things like social media management, graphic design and technical work, and answering emails. See if there are any tasks you can ask someone else to do.

In a flip, you can also outsource your kids' education. Get someone else to be in charge of supervising their school time and helping with answers. This could be a spouse, a friend, or tutor for example.

Teaching kids about business is always a good thing, so including them in what you do is an awesome learning experience. Some ways they can be involved could include labelling catalogues, packing orders, writing reviews, video editing, sorting shelves, setting up and taking down displays, helping to come up with product ideas, and more. Again, this will vary based on your business and what ages your children are. You can also just sit them beside you if you have to work on a computer — having them feel like they are important enough to be there is good too. You can even set up a special workstation nearby so they can copy what you are doing.

One frustration I've discovered as a homeschooler with a business is that although I've got big dreams and ideas, I can't accomplish them all. At least not right now. Right now, I've got children to raise, teach, and parent. That is my top priority. I've got to be willing to take things at the pace that is possible, not at the pace I dream of. It's hard at times, but I've had to learn to be willing to go slow.

Make a list of everything you need to accomplish and then just keep working. If you only have 5 minutes to do something while the kids are distracted, start on one thing until you have to stop. Then the next time you have 5 minutes, you already know what you are working on. Keep at it until that project is done, then onto the next. Chip away at the list – one thing at a time. It can be done, even if it doesn't feel as productive as a large amount of time to work.

Is there a way you can add work to tasks that don't require full attention? While the kids are playing in the backyard or settling into bed at night, can you listen to podcasts, watch videos, do social media planning, answer emails, type up outlines and ideas, or do other business-related tasks? Be productive without being chained to your desk.

The truth is that it's possible to both work and homeschool, but you need a plan that will allow for success.

YOUR ACTION STEP

If you work either at home or out of the home, consider the tips above. Work on finding solutions to help make the juggle of both important areas of your life fit together more easily.

CHAPTER TWENTY

CHOOSING EXTRA-CURRICULAR ACTIVITIES

I love travel backpacks. They can hold so much stuff. There are clips, buckles, attachments, and all kinds of pockets - some of them are even hidden so you can feel like a spy when you use them. It makes it easy to add extras to your pack: a sleeping bag roll, a water bottle, a travel mug, an umbrella, your passport and money, all your tech accessories, etc. I've even seen some that have a sleeve for your laptop!

Do you need all those extras? No. Are they fun to take with you? Absolutely. But when you live with all your belongings on your back, you realize pretty quickly that extras weigh you down. Some may be more of an essential (like a sleeping bag) so they are worth keeping around. Others can probably be left behind. Just because there are unused pockets and clips doesn't mean the backpack isn't being used to the best potential.

There is a common joke in the homeschooling world: "Why do they call it homeschooling when we are never at home!?" Although the general public tends to see home education as bubble-wrapping our kids away from the world, the reality is that there are plenty of opportunities for our kids to learn out and about. Maybe there are too many opportunities.

Extracurricular activities offer homeschoolers many benefits, primarily as an opportunity to socialize and make friends. If our children are extroverts, they thrive on interaction with others. Plus, it's a great opportunity to include topics, subjects, and activities we might be weak in or can't do at home.

But how can you avoid letting activities overrule your days?

Here are some questions to ask before signing up for activities:

- **Were any of these extra activities on your priority list?**

The first step is to go back to your priorities list that we made earlier in this book. If music is very important to you and your children, for example, giving up your music lessons probably shouldn't be an option. But if you are just doing something for the sake of doing something, ditch it. It's just sucking time away from your life.

- **How much of a time commitment will this activity require of my child and our family? Does that fit with our schedule?**

Next, look at the plan/calendar and see what you can honestly fit in. If life is already pretty busy and you are stretched thin, adding extra things will just make you more tired, more stressed, and less happy. If this activity requires large commitments of time, consider how that will impact your whole family and the other things on your priorities lists.

- **Can you afford it?**

One of the biggest challenges of doing so many extra activities is that they cost money. Sometimes, they cost a lot of money. Take a look at the program you are considering. What are their costs outside of the actual registration fee? Will you have to pay for a uniform, an instrument, trips, tools, or accessories to participate successfully? Is this within your budget?

- **Does your child want to participate in this activity?**

Sometimes, as parents, we see something we think would be fun/cool/ interesting and jump at the opportunity to participate. Then, when it's time to go, our kids balk, making us frustrated (and confused why they don't want to do the activity we were all excited about!) Talk to your kids before signing them up for things. They will tell you if they are interested or not.

The Don'ts

Don't fall into the trap that each kid needs an activity to be fair. If you have multiple children, it might seem unfair to register only one child in an activity. But it's not. Kids have different needs. Don't sign up for an activity just for the sake of having an activity. Don't look for fair. Look at each of your children separately.

Don't do something because it's "expected" of you as a homeschooler. Signing up for something just because you think that's what homeschoolers are supposed to do can lead to some very burnt out kids and parents. You don't HAVE to sign up for a co-op, or music lessons, or art class, or the local gym days. You don't HAVE to do anything. That's the beauty of homeschooling. If you've been struggling with an activity because you thought you had to... I free you from that right now. Cross it off your list.

Don't pack your days. Our local community has so many things available for homeschoolers: classes for cooking, art, gymnastics, dance, music, swimming. There are library clubs, snowboarding teams, field trips, meetups, and volunteer opportunities. We could probably be so busy every day that we would never be home. But we would be exhausted. Don't fill your days with everything. It's just too much. Create peace by not having to rush around all the time. Start with one or two and add more activities as wanted or needed. (Follow the "less is more" mentality!)

Most importantly, learn to say no and be okay with it.

I think we can too easily get sucked into all these extra things because we have a hard time letting someone down or because we feel guilty for saying no. We have to be willing to say no and then learn to be okay with that. "No" isn't a bad thing. It's very freeing because now we can be in charge of our days and our time. We can decide what is important to us and what isn't, and we can give ourselves space to breathe and relax.

YOUR ACTION STEP

Considering the questions and tips above, figure out what extracurricular activities you want to add to your homeschool year.

PART VI:

THE TOUGH STUFF

CHAPTER TWENTY-ONE
GOOD DAYS, BAD DAYS

From the outside looking in, homeschool has this rosy, dreamy glow. If you believe the blogs, the news articles, Pinterest, and the community in general, you might think perfection is the norm every day.

The truth is that, just like parenting, there are good days and there are bad days.

In an ideal world, everything just clicks together. School gets done without any arguing or complaining. You've enjoyed the day with your kids learning and playing together. The chores are all checked off the list so your house feels organized and clean. Supper is ready, the kids are playing nicely, and it feels wonderful. Just like everything you hoped it would be.

Other days, you collapse into bed feeling like you've spent the day being a punching bag. Kids have fought with each other all day long. School ended up being more of a battle than learning, and you question your sanity about whether one page of math should have been that much of a fight. You give up on supper plans and let the kids eat cereal while you try to keep your tears hidden from the kids, defeated and exhausted. You wonder if that list of reasons is strong enough to keep you on this path.

Reality is that most days fall somewhere in between - a mix of wonderful and chaos.

Although we all want good days more often than bad, there are some things we can do when we are faced with a rough homeschooling day. On those days, it's worth taking a break to do something else instead.

Take some time to:

- read aloud

- watch educational TV

- cook or bake something

- go outside to play or go for a walk

- Reset your day and start fresh tomorrow.

If you and your child are frequently not working well as a teacher and student, here are some suggestions:

- Approach learning from a different angle. Try something fresh and new. Try a different homeschool style. Get hands-on. Change things up.

- Talk to your child about the problem. Ask what you can do to work better together; their insights might surprise you.

- Look for outside resources, courses, and classes. Have someone else teach for a while to take a load off you and to let your child experience a different voice and way of teaching. There are a lot of great online classes you can take advantage of.

- Take a break. Back off the formal schooling and allow your child to explore for a while on their own. Give them learning experiences through life and play. They might learn more than you expect.

But what if, for you and your kids, things seem to be an everyday struggle, you dread getting started in the morning, frustrations outnumber the joy, and you just want to throw up the white flag in surrender?

WHAT IF HOMESCHOOLING ISN'T WORKING?

First, take a step back.

In the thick of things, it's hard to take a good, serious look at what's going on. Pull yourself out of the moment and evaluate. What is really happening here?

Are your everyday battles because you've picked a curriculum that's too hard, too boring, or too different from how your child learns? Is your child going through puberty and hormones are causing bad attitudes? Do you have expectations or standards that are too big or too high for your child? Is your child struggling to understand something but doesn't know how to articulate it?

Think about the reasons homeschooling is hard right now. Sometimes a big problem can have a fairly easy solution.

From here, it's time to consider what you can do to change this.

- Is it as simple as finding a new approach to teaching and learning?

- Could just changing to a new curriculum be effective?

- What about changing up your daily schedule or breaking up your day differently?

- What if you add a new element of fun to your days — like gamification (turning things into a game) or more outside time?

- What if, instead of doing a pre-set curriculum, you opted to study a topic your child is curious or interested in?

- Would encouraging your child with the power of independence, such as giving them a checklist to complete before a certain time, make them more willing to work?

It might be worth it to take a break from schooling for a while. Take a week, take a month, take whatever time you need to reconnect with your child one on one. Spend the time you would usually do school focused on something your child loves, like reading together, playing LEGO, watching a movie, or kicking a ball back and forth. Find something positive to do with your child instead of struggling with a constant negative.

Talk to your child. See if they can offer ideas or suggestions that might change things around. Kids often have fantastic insight and ideas. For example, I was desperately trying to find a way to encourage my boys to stay on task. I talked to my oldest and he came up with the idea of turning schooling into a "video game" — earning experience points for completing lessons and fighting a mega boss through the week by using "hit points" he earned as well. He designed a mega boss and we had a great week. Did it last forever? No. But it helped us be successful with our learning, we had fun, and it gave me ideas for the future that we can do to freshen things up if we're struggling.

WHAT IF NOTHING WORKS?

If nothing is working, or your relationship with your child is at danger of blowing up, remember this important thing: School IS an option.

You haven't failed because you've sent a child off to the classroom in your neighbourhood.

Homeschooling, no matter how appealing or ideal, is NOT the only way for your child to get an education. Your parent-child relationship, your sanity, and your child's self-esteem are far more important than homeschooling success.

It's okay to send your kid to school if it's the right decision for your family and your child.

This break from each other every day can help repair a frazzled relationship, allow you to spend more quality time and less "teaching" time together, and give your child a chance to see the difference between school at home and school at school. Even if you choose not to return to homeschooling, it's a good comparison for them to make.

Do what is right for your child. Whatever that looks like.

Remember. Relationship first.

CHAPTER TWENTY-TWO
HANDLING OPPOSITION

Choosing homeschooling as an education method can draw a lot of heat from people who don't understand exactly what you are doing. You may discover some people you encounter are prone to drilling you with questions about your choice, will argue with you about what you are doing, and flat-out refuse to accept your decision to homeschool as valid. Opposition can be unsettling, especially if you are a new homeschooler who doesn't have a solid foot on the ground yet.

There are generally two responses to situations where people get up in our faces about our homeschooling decision. The first is to let their words break in and fill us with doubt, uncertainty, and concern — undermining the decision we have carefully made. The second is the fight reaction — standing our ground with our fists clenched, ready to prove why exactly homeschooling is best.

But before we submit to flight or fight, it's important for us to understand why people oppose homeschooling so we can see the picture from their point of view.

WHY PEOPLE OPPOSE HOMESCHOOLING

It's Different.

In general, anytime something doesn't follow the traditional plan, it creates a natural oppositional and negative response. Different is scary. Different is unknown. Different is dangerous. Why? Because they don't know what to expect. It is much easier to just go along with what everyone else is doing than to do something outside the box. It's safe that way — you don't run the risk of hurting yourself or others.

They Have Preconceived Ideas of What Education Should Look Like.

Most people have this idea of what education needs to look like to be successful. They have a picture of a traditional classroom, a blackboard and desks for each child, where a trained teacher leads the lessons, following an approved set of learning outcomes in a specific order based on age and development.

If this is the picture people expect when they think of school and education, it is incredibly hard to wrap their head around the thought that it can be done differently. They can't understand how homeschooling can offer a viable and complete education if it doesn't follow the idea they have.

They Don't "Get" Homeschooling.

Unfortunately, most of mainstream society has only glimpsed homeschooling through the filtered lens of the media. The news and online world don't paint the homeschooling community in the best of light. As such, people might think of homeschoolers in stereotypes:

- religious nuts

- sheltered, unsocialized kids

- abusive parents

- educationally neglected kids

- failing kids for real life

Of course, there is always one homeschooling horror story that sticks out in their mind. Because of these negatives they see and hear, people tend to consider success stories as a fluke (even if successes are 99% of the experience from the homeschooling community!).

If they have this idea that homeschooling is only these bad and terrible things, of course they are prone to suspicions and opposition about the homeschooling experience.

WHEN THEY ARE WILLING TO LEARN & LISTEN

If the person you are talking to is open to a true discussion about homeschooling and willing to learn from you, you have a great opportunity to debunk those myths and ideas people tend to have.

Help them see past the media paintbrush and see the artwork underneath instead. Use examples from your own experiences with your kids, if possible.

Try to avoid tongue in cheek responses because, although they can be fun at times (and truthful), they aren't going to add any positive points to a debate. They won't provide an opportunity to educate people about your decision.

WHEN DEALING WITH PEOPLE WHO WON'T EVER LISTEN

There are some people who, no matter how much data, personal observation, or anecdotal evidence they are presented with, will ALWAYS oppose your decision.

Learning how to steer a conversation away from discussion about any parenting or life decision you make that brings up arguments and negativity from people is a vital skill. Set boundaries for conversations and decide to be in charge of deciding what is available for discussion and what isn't.

Often as a homeschooling parent, we want to prove we have made the right decision. The truth is, we don't need to defend our choices. We need to accept that not everyone is going to accept our decision and instead, change the conversation.

Most of the strangers and people we consider acquaintances don't need an in-depth response to their comments or questions. Frankly, it's none of their business. Engaging with a response encourages people to start a debate. Don't invite discussion if you don't want to have it.

The best plan is to change the focus of the conversation from what you aren't willing to talk about to something you are. It can be anything. Answer their question with a very short and definitive comment followed by something to change the topic. You can even default to conversations about sports or the weather as needed.

As an example, an answer to the question "What about socialization?" could be "We belong to a great homeschooling community. Man, it's hot today. I wonder what it's like in (insert random city on the other side of the country here.)"

If the person you are talking with won't change the conversation, you may need to take firmer action such as walking away, hanging up the phone call, or blocking them on social media.

There are conversations where a redirection tactic won't be enough. If these are friends or family you interact with more frequently, you will need to establish clear guidelines for yourself about what you will and will not discuss.

It is INCREDIBLY hard to set firm boundaries, especially when it comes to friends, family members, and other people you care about. Why? Because you run the risk of damaging relationships and hurting people's feelings.

Setting boundary lines makes it clear that you will not talk about this anymore. It's an important skill to have if you need to counter constant arguing and opposition to your choices. Yes, you don't want to sacrifice an important relationship, but sometimes, it is a decision you have to make to be able to move forward in your homeschooling journey with success. Putting the line there puts the onus on the other person to decide whether they want to value their relationship with you over the need to argue and debate.

If you don't want to deal with opposition or disapproval, take charge of the conversation. Don't engage on topics you don't want to.

Examples of Boundary Setting Statements

- "We know you love us and our children and want the best for us. This is the decision we have made for our family. It is not up for discussion."

- "I want us to have a good relationship. Please enjoy my children, but remember I am their parent. I make the decisions for their education. If you bring this topic up again, we will leave."

- "I know you don't understand our choice, and that's okay, but I will not have this conversation anymore. Let's talk about something else, or I will have to go."

You are not obligated to explain your choices to anyone. You are not required to convert anyone to your side or to make them the newest homeschooling cheerleader.

Set boundaries you are comfortable with. It's up to you and your responses. You will never be able to decide how other people are going to react but you can be in control of your response.

CHAPTER TWENTY-THREE

BURNOUT AND SELF-CARE

Travel backpacks are heavy. Hiking all day is hard on the feet and the legs. Nature can be cruel sometimes - bug bites, sunburn, and poison ivy wreak havoc on bodies walking through the wilderness. Blisters form on heels from the constant motion against shoes. It's important at the end of a hard day of pushing forward that you take some time to drop your pack, stretch your weary muscles, put something over the blisters, cook something over the fire, and get some rest. Stopping at camp for the night is a vital part of the journey. You need a rest and recovery period to be able to keep moving again the next day.

Experts say over and over that self-care is important for parents, especially for homeschooling parents. We are around kids essentially all day, every day. It can be exceptionally draining to us emotionally, physically, and mentally to keep up with all their needs all the time. Taking time to recharge and reset is important.

But, in a house of chaos, how can we do that as homeschoolers?

SELF-CARE IDEAS

When you hear self-care, do you imagine things like spa days or getaways? A kid-free night out? These are options, but they aren't the only (or necessary) ways to get refilled. Here are some ideas of how you can squeeze "me time" into a busy homeschool life.

The 5-minute Break

You can do a mini-power up just by taking 5 minutes to yourself whenever you need it on a busy day. Step outside and take some breaths of fresh air. If you are driving somewhere, turn off the radio and just sit in the silence. Set a timer and pop onto Facebook. Just find a short activity that gives you a minute to catch your breath and clear your head.

The 15-minute Break

Sometime in the day, I'm sure you can find 15 minutes of kid-free time. Some people like getting up before the kids, some staying up after they are in bed, and others intentionally set a time in the middle of the day. Use this time to do something that will take a little longer and can give you a much-needed pause.

Have a shower. (Maybe sing in it for extra fun!) Pray or meditate. Read a chapter of a book. Have a cup of your favourite warm drink. Lay down on the couch and power nap. Tell the kids you are on break for 15 minutes and unless there is blood or the house is on fire to leave you alone. (Bathroom doors with locks are a miracle some days!)

The 30-minute Break

If you have little ones, strap them into their stroller and, while they are contained go for a walk. You can even put a podcast or audiobook onto a mobile device and listen while you walk! Do an exercise video. Sit in the backyard and listen to the birds. Have a bubble bath. Talk to a friend. Watch a YouTube video of something you want to learn. Spend some time on your hobby.

The Longer Break

Go out for coffee with a friend. Do a mom or dad's night out. Join an adult class or study group. Go to the spa and get a manicure. Swap with another homeschool parent who will take your kids for a couple of hours one day and then you take theirs another day. If your kids are in a class or lesson, chat with other parents or curl up in the corner or car to read. After the kids are in bed, binge-watch a new or a favourite show. Go out to the movies or a play.

The Getaway

If leaving the kids at home and going away is the best way for you to fully recharge, go for it. Plan a weekend alone or with your spouse or friend. Go to a homeschool conference. Do a reverse getaway and send the kids to the grandparents' house for a night.

Finding time for self-care as a homeschooling parent doesn't mean you have to leave for long periods (but it can!). It's more about making sure you remember to put yourself and your needs in the priority spot at least once in a while. I can be horrible about this but it's important. Without a mental, physical, or emotional break from all your responsibilities and tasks, you can very quickly find yourself burnt out.

SIGNS OF BURNOUT

In the thick of it, it can be hard to look around and recognize you are heading down the path to burn out. Here are some signs to watch for:

- a feeling of dread about your homeschooling day or activities
- a short fuse, lack of patience, and feeling irritable
- waning energy
- no interest in doing activities in your homeschool that used to bring joy
- wanting to just stay home instead of going to your usual activities
- a "DONE" feeling about everything
- a lack of emotion at all
- a feeling that you are just going through the motions
- exhaustion that just won't go away
- a heavy feeling in your body
- a feeling of overwhelm or helplessness, depression, or failure
- finding yourself being critical or negative towards your children and their work

DEALING WITH BURNOUT

If you are already feeling like you've hit the wall: tired, stressed, frazzled, and at the end of your rope... there is hope.

A few years ago, I burnt out hardcore. A combination of things contributed to it, but what eventually happened was that I could barely function. My primary goals for the day were to get out of bed and make my way to my desk chair in the middle of the house where I could supervise everyone. It was impossible to focus on much and productive days were a thing of the past. I was incapable of completing even the simplest of tasks and I felt tired all day, every day. It was terrible. I hated it.

It took me months of struggling before I could add anything more than "stare blankly at the computer screen" to my to-do list and complete it. It was a slow process to get myself back into my normal routine, and even when I thought I was finally on my feet — a day would come along that just shut me down again.

Having gone through that experience taught me a hard lesson about self-care. Sometimes, we do just have to keep pushing forward and make things happen, but most of the time, we need to pay attention to ourselves and take the breaks we need when we need it.

These days, I'm much more aware of how I feel. If I'm dragging or struggling, I stop. I permit myself to take time to recharge so that I don't end up falling over the edge again.

Here are some of the tips I learned while surviving a homeschool burnout.

Tip #1: Stop

If you are feeling burnt out, it's time to stop. Cut as many projects, commitments, activities, and extras as possible. You need a break. You need to take time to recover. Get rid of (or pause) all the things that have been pulling you in many directions.

Tip #2: Simplify

Right now, if you are burnt out, strip life to the bare minimum. If you need to hide all the dishes and use paper ones... do it. Only clean the bathrooms once in a while (they will be fine — no one will die if you don't clean them every day or every week or even every couple of weeks. Trust me.) Don't answer the phone or the door if you aren't up to it. Don't set any big goals.

Tip #3: Skip School

When you are burnt out, the thought of trying to tackle anything official for school can be so overwhelming. Give yourself and your kids permission to skip school. Instead of structured learning, snuggle and read together. Use online games and activities. Watch documentaries and educational TV shows. Play board games.

Guess what? The kids will learn. They have an amazing ability to learn so much, even without us being intentional with a plan. And, if you need to... know it's okay to take a break from homeschooling and send the kids to school. You haven't failed. You are allowed to do what's best for everyone, and if that's it — do it. If you feel up to taking them out of school again in the future, you can do that. So don't sink farther into the hole because you don't want to fail at homeschooling.

Tip #4: Soothe Your Soul

Think of something that allows you to relax, recharge, and get some time to recover. Spend time doing something you love — reading, knitting, crafting, photography... whatever it is, just do it. Make sure you get a full night's sleep, eat properly, and drink lots of water. Allow yourself to indulge with limits. Have that chocolate bar you are craving or make a batch of cookies to snack on. It's not going to ruin you forever to have a cookie bingeing session.

Tip #5: Seek Support

It's hard, INCREDIBLY hard, but very important to ask for help. See if friends or family will help you with the kids, or bring you meals, or come sit to talk. Sometimes even hiring someone to babysit while you relax can give you some healing space. A nap can be a game-changer. Or hire someone to clean for you. Think of how you can use help, and ask for it. People won't know if you don't tell them.

Tip #6: Start Slowly & Set Small Goals for Success

When you are starting to feel like your head is coming above the water and you are stable again, start small. Set a goal to accomplish one thing. Don't dive back into life at full force — it will just drag you under again.

Maybe your first goal will be to have the kids add math lessons to 3 days of the week. See how that goes. Then build from there — add in more subjects and days until you are back to full school plans like you usually have. When that is going well and you feel on top of things, you can add more to life. Remember, slow is the key.

Tip #7: Step Back and See

When you have started feeling better, before committing to anything extra, step back and evaluate whether that thing needs to be a part of your life or not. Something overwhelmed you in the first place, so think about what was the straw that broke the camel's back. How can you make sure that doesn't happen again?

Being burnt out is exhausting. The thought of doing... anything... is just overwhelming. Hopefully, you can catch yourself before you get too far.

ACTION STEP

Make sure to include self-care in your day. Write down some ways you know will help you recharge.

WELCOME TO DAY ONE

You are ready to head out on your journey! You are all geared up with proper equipment. Your bag is packed with everything you need and carefully strapped to your back. You have a map and an itinerary in hand.

It's time to step out of the Canadian Homeschooling Outfitter Shop and onto the path.

Before we go, let me offer a last set of words.

Relax. When you first start homeschooling, everything is overwhelming. There is curriculum and methodology and classes and opinions and guilt and stress and questions. Just relax. Step back. There's no obligation to throw yourself into the action and do ANYTHING. Just take things slow. Take deep breaths and take the time you need to figure things out.

Play. Even when it doesn't "feel" like it, it's important to remember that play IS learning. It's not wasted time. It's vital. So, let them play. Or, better yet, get down on the floor and join them.

Ask. Reference the people who are already ahead of you on your journey. Pick their brains for experience and wisdom. Find out what worked and didn't work with their family. Ask about local activities, conferences, support systems. Their knowledge is invaluable. Be sure to ask more than one person, as everyone's homeschooling experience is different.

Believe. You need to feel passionate about this choice. People who don't know about homeschooling are likely to question you, repeatedly. If you don't know why are you are doing this, it can be easy to feel belittled or guilt-ridden. You need to have a strong will and determination to make it work. Faith in yourself and the choices you make goes a long way to success.

Support. Find people who will come alongside you on your journey. A local homeschool group, friends and family who want to encourage you, an online community who can answer any question you throw at them — these are just a few examples of support systems you can (and should!) tap into.

Network. Get to know the people, businesses, and online communities that are relevant to homeschooling. Building a network means you have people to back you up but also that you have answers at your fingertips — maybe even discounts or places to trade products. You never know the full benefits of networking until you need to ask for something!

Listen. Hear what your child is saying, asking, and wondering. The off-handed, but sincerely curious questions of a child can lead to amazing learning experiences. Follow their lead, even if you are following a set curriculum. There's always a teaching opportunity based on their passions and questions. Things we learn when we are interested stick with us much longer than things we learned because we had to.

Learn. Be a good role model; always be learning yourself, even if that's as simple as learning alongside them. Maybe math has always been your struggle — use this opportunity to work on strengthening your skills. Or maybe you've always wanted to learn how to crochet or play the piano or write a book. Take the time to do that now with your children watching. Teach them the skills to find out how to learn anything they want. Take baby steps together.

Enjoy. Don't spend all your time stressing out or researching or feeling guilty. Enjoy this experience as much as you can. Savour the look of understanding when it lights up your child's eyes. Soak up the love as they cuddle with you while you read aloud. Giggle with them when they find something funny or do something wrong resulting in hilarity. Be a cheerleader for their success and remind yourself that this time is short — even if it feels like it's lasting forever.

All right. I think you are set. Let me just grab my compass and we'll be on our way together.

COMMON HOMESCHOOL TERMS

Whenever you join a new community, you hear words you aren't familiar with. It's the same with homeschooling. There are many terms homeschoolers use frequently that you might not recognize. Here is a quick reference of some popular ones.

Association: Typically a volunteer organization intended to advocate for and support homeschoolers within their province or territory.

Boxed Curriculum: An all-in-one homeschool curriculum package for a single grade from a single publisher.

Co-op: A homeschool group that meets together regularly to share the responsibility of education through classes generally taught by parents of the children in the group.

Copywork: Where a student copies a portion of text from a book to practice handwriting.

Deschooling: A period of time between pulling a child out of a school and starting homeschooling, where you intentionally steer clear of academics to reset your mindset about what education needs to be like. It's kind of like school detox.

Dual Enrollment: When high school students take college courses to earn credit for both college and high school at the same time.

Freeschooling (*also called unschooling*): A homeschool method that uses a child-led, life learning approach without curriculum or a learning plan.

Lapbook: A file folder that contains "mini-books" or other paper foldables glued on the inside with information on various parts of a single topic.

Living Books: Typically a book written in a narrative style that engages the reader's interest and imagination.

Looping: A schedule that, instead of having specific tasks occur on a specific day or at a specific time, uses a list of what comes next to be repeated at completion.

Manipulatives: Small tools, toys, or resources to be used, usually for mathematics, to visualize problems.

Mastery: An approach where a subject is studied in-depth and at length until it has been fully understood.

Morning Basket: A collection of activities or lessons intended to be done as a group learning time. Sometimes called circle time.

Narration: A passage of a book is read out loud, then the child repeats back what they heard in their own words.

Notebooking: A method of taking notes that is kind of like journaling and can include whatever you would like to — drawings, maps, notes, etc.

Piecemeal: Instead of planning things out in full, this approach plans out things little by little as they go.

Scope and Sequence: The plan for the order of what a curriculum covers.

Secular: A worldview that has no religious or spiritual basis.

Spine: This is the primary resource or reference - typically a book — around which learning takes place.

Spiral: A method of learning where a subject is taught and then revisited with a newer layer of complexity over and over until mastered.

Strewing: Laying resources and books around for your child to engage with at their own interest.

Twaddle: Things that fill up time without value — trivial or foolish resources, like abridged books instead of classics.

Workboxes: A method where each activity or lesson for the day is placed into its own box, so a child can complete a task and then move onto the next one through their school day.

You will also find most associations are referenced by acronyms, such as:

BCHEA : British Columbia Home Education Association

OCHEC: Ontario Christian Home Educator's Connection

MASH: Manitoba Association for Schooling at Home

SHBE: Saskatchewan Home Based Educators

AHEA: Alberta Home Education Association

Many popular curricula are also known by their acronyms as well, like:

MUS : Math-U-See

SOS: Switched-On Schoolhouse

IEW: Institute for Excellence in Writing

EIW: Essentials in Writing

HWT: Handwriting without Tears

TT: Teaching Textbooks

LOF: Life of Fred

AAS/AAR: All About Spelling / All About Reading

SOTW: Story of the World

MOH: Mystery of History

ACE: Accelerated Christian Education

CLE: Christian Light Education

FIAR: Five in a Row

BJU: Bob Jones University

OM: Oak Meadow

INDEX

NEED MORE HELP?

My mission is to connect homeschoolers across Canada with each other and with resources to help them on their journey. Here's how I do that:

- **The Canadian Homeschooler Website:** This is where you can find posts with tips and information, reviews, booklists, curriculum ideas, and much more --> thecanadianhomeschooler.com

- **The Learning Centre:** This is where you can find free printables, videos, ebooks, and more. --> shop.thecanadianhomeschooler.com/library

- **The Canadian Homeschooler Facebook Page**: This is where you can find me hanging out online, sharing resources, and having conversations. --> facebook.com/thecanadianhomeschooler

- **Canadian Homeschool Community:** This is where you can find support and encouragement with other homeschoolers and myself, training videos, and online activities --> canadianhomeschoolcommunity.com

- **Canadian Online Homeschool Conference**: This is where you can find an annual conference full of wise and experienced speakers from across Canada --> canadianhomeschoolconference.com

ABOUT THE AUTHOR

Lisa Marie Fletcher is the voice behind the website, The Canadian Homeschooler – a popular first stop for parents looking for help getting started with homeschooling and for those searching for Canadian homeschooling resources. More than a decade of teaching five children at home has given her plenty of experience on the path. Lisa Marie lives in Ontario, Canada. Visit her website at thecanadianhomeschooler.com

Made in the USA
Monee, IL
26 May 2021